Filling
Words
with
LIGHT

Other Jewish Lights Books by Lawrence Kushner

The Book of Letters: A Mystical Hebrew Alphabet

The Book of Words: Talking Spiritual Life, Living Spiritual Talk

Eyes Remade for Wonder: A Lawrence Kushner Reader

God Was in This Place & I, i Did Not Know:
Finding Self, Spirituality and Ultimate Meaning

Honey from the Rock: An Introduction to Jewish Mysticism

Invisible Lines of Connection: Sacred Stories of the Ordinary

Jewish Spirituality: A Brief Introduction for Christians

The River of Light: Jewish Mystical Awareness

The Way Into Jewish Mystical Tradition

For Children

Because Nothing Looks Like God with Karen Kushner

The Book of Miracles: A Young Person's Guide to
Jewish Spiritual Awareness

How Does God Make Things Happen? with Karen Kushner
(SkyLight Paths Publishing)

What Does God Look Like? with Karen Kushner
(SkyLight Paths Publishing)

Where Is God? with Karen Kushner
(SkyLight Paths Publishing)

Five Cities of Refuge: Weekly Reflections on Genesis, Exodus,
Leviticus, Numbers, and Deuteronomy
with David Mamet (Schocken)

Other Books by Nehemia Polen

The Rebbe's Daughter: Memoir of a Hasidic Childhood
(Jewish Publication Society)

The Holy Fire: The Teaching of Rabbi Kalonymus Kalman
Shapira, the Rebbe of the Warsaw Ghetto
(Jason Aronson)

Filling Words with LIGHT

Hasidic and Mystical Reflections on Jewish Prayer

LAWRENCE KUSHNER
NEHEMIA POLEN

JEWISH LIGHTS Publishing
Woodstock, Vermont

Filling Words with Light:
Hasidic and Mystical Reflections on Jewish Prayer

2004 First Printing
© 2004 by Lawrence Kushner and Nehemia Polen

Library of Congress Cataloging-in-Publication Data
Kushner, Lawrence, 1943–
Filling words with light : Hasidic and mystical reflections on Jewish prayer / Lawrence Kushner, Nehemia Polen.
p. cm.
ISBN 1-58023-216-7 (hardcover)
1. Judaism—Liturgy—Texts—History and criticism. 2. Jewish meditations. 3. Hasidism. 4. Mysticism—Judaism. 5. Spiritual life—Judaism. I. Polen, Nehemia. II. Title.
BM660.K88 2004
296.4'5—dc22

2004015897

10 9 8 7 6 5 4 3 2 1

Manufactured in Canada.
Jacket and Interior Design: Lawrence Kushner.

This book and its jacket were designed by the author. For the interior, the text face is Minion, the display font is John Handy, and the Hebrew is Davka's Keren. For the jacket design, the display fonts are Ellington and John Handy.

Published by Jewish Lights Publishing
A Division of LongHill Partners, Inc.
Sunset Farm Offices, Route 4, P.O. Box 237
Woodstock, VT 05091
Tel: (802) 457-4000   Fax: (802) 457-4004
www.jewishlights.com

For Zalman Schachter-Shalomi, our teacher,

who showed our generation how to weave

the flowers of the field into garlands.

Contents

3. The Shema and Its Blessings
שמע וברכותיה Shema U'virkhoteha

4. The Standing Prayer
עמידה Amidah

7. The Sabbath
שבת Shabbat

Introduction

צֹהַר תַּעֲשֶׂה לַתֵּבָה

Make a window for the ark;
Put a skylight in your words.

Perhaps one of the most important metaphors for the words of prayer in Jewish tradition comes to us in the name of the Baal Shem Tov in his *Tsava'at Harivash* (76). Like most such insights in Judaism, this one blossoms from a nuanced reading of a biblical verse—in the case before us, a double entendre on God's instructions to Noah about how to build the ark: "YOU SHALL MAKE A SKYLIGHT FOR THE ARK; FINISH IT WITHIN ONE CUBIT OF THE TOP; MAKE A DOOR FOR THE ARK ON ITS SIDE; MAKE IT WITH LOWER, SECOND, AND THIRD LEVELS" (Gen. 6:16).

Noting that the Hebrew word for ark, *teivah,* can also mean "word" and that the Hebrew word for window, *tsohar,* can also mean "to shine," the BeShT teaches that every word in prayer a person utters should radiate light. It should have a skylight.

We must remember, he continues, that every Hebrew letter resembles a person, with a body, a personality, and a spark of the Divine. And, like a person, these letters all yearn to join with others in holiness. In this way the letters become fused, one by one, into words and the words into sentences. One must therefore put one's entire soul into every prayerful utterance and thereby help the letters join into words and raise oneself in great and unending joy …

And just how could a human being accomplish such a daunting and holy task? We read in Genesis 7:1 that "YOU AND ALL YOUR HOUSEHOLD SHALL ENTER THE ARK/WORD." This teaches, says the Baal Shem, that you must put your whole body and soul into the words of your prayer.

This book is neither a prayer book nor a commentary on the liturgy; as its subtitle implies, it is an anthology of reflections—meditations and interpretations on Jewish liturgy that we have found to be insightful, surprising, and wise. Students seeking a more comprehensive treatment of contemplative prayer in Hasidism are urged to consult Arthur Green and Barry Holtz's excellent *Your Word Is Fire: The Hasidic Masters on Contemplative Prayer* (Woodstock, VT: Jewish Lights, 1993); and, for those desiring a more systematic, academic treatment, we highly recommend Louis Jacobs's definitive *Hasidic Prayer* (New York: Schocken, 1973).

We have tried, wherever possible without distorting the original meaning of the biblical or liturgical text, to offer translations that are gender-neutral. In any case, the translations are never offered as literal but, instead, as renditions of the phrase in its context. To help the reader more easily recognize biblical citations, we have set them all in small capital letters. Finally, all references to the *shem ham'forash,* the ineffable name of God, *yod, heh, vav,* and *heh,* and its common liturgical euphemism, *yod, yod* (customarily rendered as "the Lord"), are translated as "Adonai."

With a few exceptions, we have listed our reflections in the order in which they appear in the traditional liturgy. We have placed the comments on the Sabbath insertions (4.6, 4.7) during the weekday *Amidah* and *L'khah Dodi* (7.2, 7.5) as part of Shabbat at home. We have also included *Adonai, Adonai* (5.2) from the High Holy Day liturgy within the regular Torah service. *Tachanun* (6.1–6.4) traditionally precedes the reading of the Torah, but we have grouped it along with *Alenu* and *Kaddish* instead. And, in a few places, we have included passages unique to the Sephardic (Spanish-Portuguese) rite.

This book owes its existence to Rabbi Lawrence Hoffman and Stuart M. Matlins, editor in chief and publisher of Jewish Lights, for two reasons. Back in 1995 they had the vision of creating a multivolume, annotated siddur (Jewish prayer book). Now, the *My People's Prayer Book* series is a reality. First, we want to express our gratitude to them for their invitation to write the mystical-Hasidic commentary for this remarkable series, and now we want also to thank them for their generous permission to be able to publish those contributions as this stand-alone volume. And, of course, we also want to express our gratitude to Jewish Lights Publishing's wonderful staff, especially Jon Sweeney and Emily Wichland, for their vision, patience, and enthusiasm.

In the pages that follow, we have assembled what we hope the reader will agree are a bouquet of interpretations, comments, stories, and reflections on how to put more of oneself into the words of one's prayer; how to give them new life; how to en-spirit them; how to *fit them* with their own individual skylights, or, if you will, in the imagery of the title of this volume, how one might begin *filling words with light*.

On the Shabbat when we read: "THESE ARE THE WORDS...."

    L. K.
    San Francisco

    N. P.
    Boston

1

The Blessings of Morning

ברכות השחר

Birkhot Hashachar

We hope that you will enjoy this book and find it useful in enriching your life.

Book title: _____

Your comments: _____

How you learned of this book: _____

Reasons why you bought this book: (check all that apply)

❑ ATTRACTIVE INSIDE ❑ RECOMMENDATION OF FRIEND ❑ SUBJECT ❑ AUTHOR ❑ ATTRACTIVE COVER

If purchased: Bookseller _____ City _____ ❑ RECOMMENDATION OF REVIEWER ❑ GIFT

State _____

Please send me a JEWISH LIGHTS Publishing catalog. I am particularly interested in: (check all that apply)

1. ❑ Spirituality
2. ❑ Mysticism
3. ❑ Philosophy/Theology
4. ❑ History/Politics

5. ❑ Women's Issues
6. ❑ Environmental Issues
7. ❑ Healing/Recovery
8. ❑ Children's Books

9. ❑ Caregiving/Grieving
10. ❑ Ideas for Adult Reading Groups
11. ❑ Religious Education Resources
12. ❑ Audio Tapes of Author Lectures

Name (PRINT) _____

Street _____

City _____ State _____ Phone _____

Please send a JEWISH LIGHTS Publishing catalog to my friend:

Name (PRINT) _____

E-mail _____

City _____ State _____ Zip _____

Street _____

Phone _____

Name (PRINT) _____

Street _____

City _____ State _____ Zip _____

JEWISH LIGHTS PUBLISHING

Sunset Farm Offices, Rte. 4 • P.O. Box 237 • Woodstock, VT 05091 • Tel. (802) 457-4000 Fax: (802) 457-4004

Available at better booksellers. Visit us online at www.jewishlights.com

JEWISH LIGHTS PUBLISHING
SUNSET FARM OFFICES RTE 4
PO BOX 237
WOODSTOCK VT 05091-0237

1.1 Awakening

יִתְגַּבֵּר כָּאֲרִי לַעֲמֹד
בַּבֹּקֶר לַעֲבוֹדַת בּוֹרְאוֹ

*Rouse yourself each morning
like a lion to serve your Creator.*

"Rouse yourself each morning like a lion to serve your Creator." With these words, Joseph Caro (1488–1575) commences his *Shulchan Arukh,* the definitive code of Jewish law. Written originally for Sephardi Jewish praxis, the *Shulchan Arukh,* or "Set Table," did not specifically address the needs of Ashkenazim. Then, between 1569 and 1571, Moses Isserles (1530–1572) published his commentary, the *Mapa* or "Tablecloth," for German Jews with the *Shulchan Arukh.* The *Mapa* opens with Psalm 16:8, "CONTINUALLY, I SET ADONAI BEFORE ME ..." Taken together, Nosson Sternhartz of Nemirov, in his *Likkutei Halakhot,* suggests that the opening lines of each text, "Rouse yourself each morning like a lion ..." and "CONTINUALLY SET ADONAI BEFORE YOU ...," describe the paradigm of awakening: like a lion in service of God, who is ever before you.

Sternhartz cites his master, Nachman of Breslov (1772–1810), who warns that too much self-examination and introspection will inevitably create anxiety over your distance from God. Such preoccupation with your defects

3

only leads to depression. And, since when you are depressed you are effectively incapacitated and unable to serve your Creator, sadness of any kind is an enemy of right acting. You must therefore continually strive, counsels Nachman, to find something good in yourself. Always be on guard against the arguments of the insidious inner voice trying to persuade you that you're no damn good, that you've never done anything of value, that even the good you've attempted is defective. This is the voice of the enemy.

Your most effective defense is the simple fact that it's inconceivable you don't have *some* good points. Find one, advises Nachman; then find another. Keep looking. Begin by giving yourself the benefit of the doubt. Of course you've made mistakes; nevertheless, by adding one good point to another, you gradually move from self-deprecation to self-respect. And only through such self-affirmation will you merit to make *teshuvah*, "return" to God. (Indeed, one old tradition counsels that if your atonement leaves you feeling bad, then it was not *real* atonement.)

It is with this in mind that we now understand Psalm 37:10, V'OD M'AT V'EIN RASHA, "YET A LITTLE BIT MORE AND THE WICKEDNESS [the wicked dimension of your psyche] … WILL BE GONE." In other words, if you acknowledge within yourself even the littlest bit of good (that *od*, that "yet-ness"), you will no longer think yourself wicked. And once that happens, you will be able to raise yourself in joy—now finally able to pray. And this, in turn, is confirmed in Psalm 146:2, AZAMRAH LEILOHI B'ODI, literally, "I will sing to God with my *'yetness.'*" By means of just that littlest bit of "yet," you will be able to sing praises to God. (Nosson Sternhartz pushes the implication to teach that only someone who learned how to find good points— even in someone else who may be a sinner—is qualified to lead the congregation in prayer.)

And this then is how you will rouse yourself from sleep and begin each new day. Sleep, according to Sternhartz, is not unconsciousness but a metaphor for the stupor of thinking you're no damn good—and neither is anyone else. You must roar like a lion for the goodness you will find in yourself and others (based on Nachman of Breslov's *Likkutei Moharan,* 282). And now you are ready to serve God and start your day.

1.2 Gratitude

מוֹדֶה אֲנִי לְפָנֶיךָ, מֶלֶךְ חַי וְקַיָּם

I gratefully acknowledge before You,
O living and eternal King.

Abraham Isaac Kook (1865–1935), in his commentary on the prayer book *Olat Reaiyah,* notes that this first morning manifestation of our joy at being alive is an expression of gratitude. The purpose of the meditation thus is *both* acknowledgment *and* thanksgiving. They dovetail each other. Our normal experience of waking is typically accompanied by what Kook calls a turbid consciousness—a lack of focus or mild confusion. For this reason, the first word of the *Modeh* is designed to initiate a different mode of consciousness, one of wonder and gratitude for the creation of this new day, a joie de vivre. We awaken to a world filled with goodness that summons us to find the same within ourselves.

1.3 Tents of Jacob

מַה טֹּבוּ אֹהָלֶיךָ יַעֲקֹב,
מִשְׁכְּנֹתֶיךָ יִשְׂרָאֵל

HOW BEAUTIFUL ARE YOUR TENTS, O JACOB,
YOUR DWELLING PLACES, O ISRAEL. (Numbers 24:5)

Puzzled by the positioning of *Mah Tovu* at the very beginning of the morning liturgy, Karen Kushner once offered the following observation. Obviously, from this verse's original context in Numbers 24:5, the non-Jewish prophet Balaam, confronted with an array of the encamped tribes of Israel spread out before him, speaks it as a poem of praise: "All the Jews are together, and the scene is wonderful to behold." But there is something more. We might also understand the imagery of *Mah Tovu* in light of what is physically happening in the prayer hall at the time of its recitation. Everyone is putting on his or her *tallit*. And this ritual customarily begins by draping the entire prayer shawl *over one's head*. But, since everyone is busy with his or her own private ritual, people rarely have an opportunity to survey the entire scene. To someone watching it (from above), however, all those Jews would appear to have literally made their own personal tents! "HOW BEAUTIFUL ARE YOUR TENTS, O JACOB!"

1.4 The Manner of Arabs

יַעֲלֶה הַכַּנְפוֹת עַל צַוָּארוֹ
וְיִתְעַטֵּף כְּעֲטִיפַת יִשְׁמְעֵאלִים

Lift up the corners [of your tallit] around your neck
and enwrap yourself in the manner of Arabs.

The following *tallit* meditation is not included in the standard prayer book. It was written by Israel Meir Hakohen Kagan (1838–1933), known also as the Hafetz Hayim, and appears in his *Mishnah Berurayh* (4), which in turn comments on the *Shulchan Arukh, Orach Hayim* (8). There we read that "at the moment of actual enwrapping the *tallit*, you cover your head until the *tallit* reaches your mouth and then you throw the four corners [around your neck and] over your left shoulder [effectively making the *tallit* into a sack covering your head] for a few seconds."

Some even go so far as to say that *this* act itself constitutes fulfillment of the commandment "to enwrap one's self with *tsitsit* [or fringes]." Others say that this making a sack of one's *tallit* is done in the "manner of Arabs [protecting themselves from wind-driven sand]." Commenting on the above, Gedalyah Fleer, a Breslover Hasid in Jerusalem, suggests that when the *tallit* is made into such a sack over your head it is an especially appropriate time to pray for the well-being of others, a time uniquely suited to the channeling of grace and healing.

1.5 Fringes

וְצִוָּנוּ לְהִתְעַטֵּף בַּצִּיצִת

And commanded us to enwrap ourselves in fringes.

Yechiel Yehoshua ben Yerachmiel Tzvi of Biala, a descendant of the Yehudi Hakadosh of Przysucha, in his *Siddur Helkat Yehoshua* (50), speaks of the intense spiritual intimacy of the moment of enwrapping oneself with the fringes of the *tallit* and offers a meditation of great contemporary relevance. It begins, as is frequently the case, with an image of *yihud*, or unification of the broken letters of God's name.

"For the sake of unifying the 'Holy One' [the *sefirah* of *Tiferet*] with God's '*Shekhinah*,' indwelling Presence [the *sefirah* of *Malkhut*], in reverence and love, and love and reverence [i.e., both ways] to unify the *yod* and the *hey* [i.e., the first two letters] of God's ineffable name with the *vav* and the *hey* [the last two letters] into a complete unity, in the name of all Israel, in order to bring pleasure to my Creator: Behold, I now enwrap my body in fringes...."

According to *gematria* (the system of assigning a numerical value to each Hebrew letter according to its sequence in the alphabet) *tsitsit* has the numerical equivalence of 600 (*tsadi* 90 + *yod* 10 + *tsadi* 90 + *yod* 10 + *tav* 400), plus the 8 strings in each bundle and 5 knots on each bundle total 613, the traditional number of commandments in the Torah (see Rashi on Numbers 15:39). So may I too enwrap my soul—my 248 limbs and 365 sinews (also totaling 613)—in the effulgence of the 613 supernal fringes.

"And just as I cover myself with a *tallit* in this world, so may I be worthy of the vestment (*haluka*) of the rabbis and deserve a beautiful *tallit* in the world-to-come, in Eden. Through this performance of the commandment to enwrap myself with *tsitsit* (fringes), may my spirit, my breath, and my soul and the words of my prayer be protected from impure and foreign influence. May my *tallit* spread her wings over my soul like an eagle covering the young in her nest with her wings" (Deut. 32:11, Song of Moses, referring to God's protection of the Jewish people in history: "AS AN EAGLE STIRS OVER HER NEST AND HOVERS IN PROTECTION OVER HER YOUNG").

1.6 A Sign on Your Hand

וּקְשַׁרְתָּם לְאוֹת עַל יָדֶךָ,
וְהָיוּ לְטֹטָפֹת בֵּין עֵינֶיךָ

*AND YOU SHALL BIND THEM FOR A SIGN ON YOUR HAND
AND THEY SHALL BE BOXES BETWEEN YOUR EYES.*
(Deuteronomy 6:8)

Rabbi Yechiel Yehoshua ben Yerachmiel Tzvi of Biala, in his *Siddur Helkat Yehoshua* (55), offers a spiritual explanation for the commandment to wrap *tefillin* on our arms. Doing so, he suggests, literally guards us against sin. The imprint of the leather strap wrapped around our arms commonly remains on our skin for hours after the strap has been removed. This impression remains as a tangible—literally in-our-flesh—reminder preventing our left hand from committing sin. (This, of course, might be an expression of Western culture's identification of the left side with evil. In French, the word for left is *gauche;* in Latin, it is *sinistra.* But the symbolism is nevertheless powerful.) As we commence our morning prayers, we stand before God with that potentially dangerous left side now literally bridled, its energy thoroughly harnessed and ready to serve the Creator.

Others have found in the placement of the arm's box on the same level with the heart an association with the

11

passage in Talmud Yerushalmi (Berakhot 9a) where God says, "Give me your heart." And likewise, the placement of the box in the center of the forehead seems to physically allude to the third eye, classically the organ of spiritual vision. In this way, setting *tefillin* "FOR A SIGN ON YOUR HAND ... AND BOXES BETWEEN YOUR EYES" (Deut. 6:8) every day gives us power to marshal both our external and internal forces for God's service. By harnessing our physical power, directing our consciousness, and focusing our spiritual vision, we commence each weekday focused on God as the ultimate force and power in the universe. And just as we, Israel, bind ourselves to the divine Presence, so may the Holy One bind Godself to the community of Israel. Indeed, we learn in Berakhot 6a that God too wears *tefillin*. But inside God's *tefillin*, instead of passages proclaiming God's uniqueness, are the words: "WHO IS LIKE YOUR PEOPLE ISRAEL, A NATION UNIQUE ON EARTH." (1 Chron. 17:21).

1.7 The Human Body

יָצַר אֶת הָאָדָם בְּחָכְמָה

You form the human body in wisdom.

In addition to the obvious and healthy acknowledgment of the mystery of the physical body's organic processes, Jewish spiritual tradition also finds in this benediction the theme of our interaction with the outside world. In other words, it's more than merely organs that are open and closed; it's also a matter of what is inside and outside. More than the body's internal rhythms, we are encouraged to contemplate how what is inside the body gets outside and vice versa. How do we enter into life-sustaining intercourse with the outside world while still maintaining a physiological boundary?

We read in *Genesis Rabbah* 1:3: "Rabbi Tanchuma opened his teaching by citing Psalm 86:10, 'FOR YOU ARE GREAT AND YOU DO WONDROUS THINGS....' Rabbi Tanchum ben Rabbi Chiya said that if a goatskin bag has a hole, even one as small as the eye of a needle, all its air escapes; yet though a person is formed with many different orifices, the person's breath does not escape through them. Who achieved this? As the psalm verse concludes, 'ONLY YOU GOD!'"

Moses Isserles, in his commentary on the "Laws of Washing Hands in the Morning" (6) of the *Shulchan*

Arukh, speaks of the mystery of life. While in utero, the mouth, for instance, must be closed, but upon birth, it must be opened or we would perish. There seems to be a kind of reversal of fetal openings and closings necessary for the maintenance of human life. In the final analysis, a human being bears humbling similarities to a goatskin sack filled with wind, a bag of breath. God graciously keeps enough breath or spirit within the body to sustain it. Thus the daily continuation of life is even more than just openings and closings, or delicate organic balance; life is a matter of getting the right things into the body and the right things out of the body and all in the proper order. For this reason, says Isserles, the blessing concludes with an image of God as wondrous healer.

1.8 Apertures and Organs

וּבָרָא בוֹ נְקָבִים נְקָבִים,
חֲלוּלִים חֲלוּלִים

And You have created in the human body
many openings and ducts.

We read in the popular Hasidic manual of spiritual discipline *Tsava'at Harivash* (22), attributed to the Baal Shem Tov: "Let whatever you experience remind you of the Holy One. If love, let it remind you of the love of God, if fear, let it remind you of the fear of God. When you go to sleep, think, my consciousness is now going to God. Even when you use the toilet, you should think, 'I am now separating bad from good. Now only the good remains for the service of God.' In this way you will be strengthened in your service of God. And just this is the real meaning of the spiritual-meditative practices known as *yihudim*, or 'unifications,' the joining of deed to God."

In earlier kabbalistic traditions *yihudim* had meant unifying the potencies of different and often arcane divine names. Here, however, we encounter an example of Hasidism's revolutionary dimension. *Yihudim* in the above passage have now become exercises of meditative awareness that bring every aspect of life—even bodily functions!—into the realm of the sacred. Everything is part of the universal divine organism. Through such *yihudim*—unifying meditations—even the most ordinary and filthy aspects of life become potentially sacred deeds.

1.9 Sweet in Our Mouths

וְהַעֲרֶב־נָא יְיָ אֱלֹהֵינוּ
אֶת־דִּבְרֵי תוֹרָתְךָ בְּפִינוּ
וּבְפִי עַמְּךָ בֵּית יִשְׂרָאֵל

*Adonai, our God, may the words of your Torah
be sweet in our mouths and
in the mouth of your people, the house of Israel.*

Yaakov Yosef of Polnoye, a second-generation Hasidic master (d. 1782), offers a parable (*Toldot Yakov Yosef, Sh'elah,* 172) to help us read the words of Torah so as to make them "sweet in our mouths." He draws on one of the most fundamental principles of Jewish spirituality: doing a sacred deed *lishmah,* "for its own sake," purely and simply in response to a divine request. Indeed, as we see in the following teaching, not only do we sweeten the sacred words of scripture, we literally liberate the letters themselves and return them to their divine source or root.

"It once happened that some travelers lost their way and decided to go to sleep until someone came along who could show them the way. Someone first came along and led them to a place of wild beasts and brigands, but then someone else came and showed them the right path. It is the same way with the letters of the Torah, through which the world was created. They came to this world in the form of travelers who have lost their way and fallen asleep. When someone comes along and studies Torah for its own sake, such a one leads them on the right path so that they can cleave to their root."

1.10 No Fixed Measure

אֵלּוּ דְבָרִים שֶׁאֵין לָהֶם שִׁעוּר

These are the things that have no fixed measure.
(Mishnah, Peah 1:1)

"The corners of the field, the first fruits, the pilgrimage offerings...." Yehuda Aryeh Leib of Ger (d. 1905), in his *Sefat Emet* (s.v. *Pesach*), explains that the sense of the divine Presence during the time of the pilgrimage festival offerings in the Temple was beyond measure. The holiness of the festival bestowed blessing upon what the *Sefat Emet* identifies as the three primary modes of all being: space *(makom)*, time *(zeman)*, and consciousness *(nefesh)*. (Indeed, this tripartite scheme goes all the way back to *Sefer Yetsirah*, one of the earliest Jewish mystical texts, dating from the first or second century.) Hagigah 2a discusses pilgrims who come to fulfill the mitzvah of being seen at the Temple with the words the following maxim: "Just as the One [God]comes to see, so the One [God] comes to be seen." This may also be read reflexively: You may come to give, but you wind up receiving. Thus in the Temple, the spiritual center of the universe, holiness radiates outward in all directions, especially during the time of festival offerings. In this way, with the right preparation and prayer, one can access this source of infinite sanctity. It has no fixed measure.

1.11 Acts of Love

וּתְגַמְּלֵנוּ חֲסָדִים טוֹבִים:
בָּרוּךְ אַתָּה יְיָ , גּוֹמֵל חֲסָדִים טוֹבִים
לְעַמּוֹ יִשְׂרָאֵל:

And You perform for us acts of good love.
Holy One of blessing, who performs acts of good love
for your people Israel.

Meshullam Zusya of Anipol (d. 1800) is puzzled by the apparent redundancy of *chasadim*, which means "love," and *tovim*, which means "good." Surely, if we receive love, then it is also obviously good. One explanation, suggests Zusya, might be to consider the case of a precious stone densely wrapped in thorns and thistles. Any attempt even to touch the jewel would scratch one's hand. The gem might be beautiful, but its covering renders it effectively useless, worthless. It is often the same way with love. For this reason, we pray not only to receive love but that the love should be clothed in goodness, in a way that it is accessible (*Bet Aharon; Yesod Ha'avodah*, 6).

1.12 Sacrifices

וְהֵרִים אֶת־הַדֶּשֶׁן אֲשֶׁר תֹּאכַל
הָאֵשׁ אֶת־הָעֹלָה

*[THE PRIEST] SHALL REMOVE THE ASHES TO WHICH THE FIRE
HAS REDUCED THE SACRIFICE.* (Leviticus 6:3)

Yehuda Aryeh Leib of Ger (d. 1905), in his *Sefat Emet* (s.v.
Tsav, 5635) offers this teaching about sacrifices. He cites
the beginning of *Parashat Tsav,* which deals almost exclu-
sively with the laws of burnt offerings: "THIS THE RITUAL OF
THE BURNT OFFERING: ... [THE PRIEST] SHALL REMOVE THE
ASHES...." How strange, notes the Gerer, that the law of
the burnt offering should *begin* with the removal of the
ashes of the *preceding* day's sacrifices. This also implies
that *every* sacrifice depends on the removal of ashes.

He then cites a teaching (*Leviticus Rabbah* 7:3) that
sacrifices make atonement for the evil meditations of our
hearts. Sacrifice represents the obliteration of sin. All that
remains are ashes, but these remnants of evil—purified
through conflagration—are now themselves good. In the
kabbalistic maxim, every descent [into sin] involves a
complementary ascent [into holiness]. Everything—even
what first seems evil—must therefore also be part of God's
creation. As Isaiah says, God creates light *and* darkness. In
this way, through the act of burning, evil is transformed

21

into good. Thus the goal of the sacrificial act has been attained. These ashes, these remnants of our evil machinations, have now themselves become holy. For this reason, they precede each day's offering. Indeed, the residue of sins now atoned is the first and highest order of spiritual business.

1.13 Rabbi Ishmael

רַבִּי יִשְׁמָעֵאל אוֹמֵר, בִּשְׁלֹשׁ עֶשְׂרֵה
מִדּוֹת הַתּוֹרָה נִדְרֶשֶׁת בָּהֶן

*Rabbi Ishmael says that according to thirteen principles
is the Torah interpreted.*

Elimelekh of Lizhensk (in *Noam Elimelekh, Likkutei
Shoshana,* 5755) is struck by the fact that thirteen is the
number of principles through which the Torah may be
interpreted and the number of divine attributes as enu-
merated in Exodus 34:5–7: "AND ADONAI DESCENDED IN THE
CLOUD, AND STOOD WITH HIM [MOSES] THERE, AND PRO-
CLAIMED THE NAME OF ADONAI. AND ADONAI PASSED BY
BEFORE HIM, AND PROCLAIMED, [1] *ADONAI,* [2] *ADONAI* [3]
GOD, [4] *MERCIFUL AND* [5] *GRACIOUS,* [6] *LONG SUFFERING,
AND* [7] *ABUNDANT IN GOODNESS AND* [8] *TRUTH,* [9] *KEEPING
MERCY FOR THOUSANDS,* [10] *FORGIVING INIQUITY AND* [11]
TRANSGRESSION AND [12] *SIN, AND THAT WILL* ... [13] *CLEAR* ..."
(italics ours). It should be noted that in the phrase selected
by the liturgy, the preceding are only attributes of love,
compassion, and mercy, whereas mention of judgment,
punishment, and anger from the rest of the biblical passage is omitted.

Rabbi Elimelekh of Lizhensk suggests that only a person who lives by these thirteen divine attributes is able to

properly interpret Torah according to Rabbi Ishmael's thirteen principles. Indeed, such an interpretation of Torah based only on love and mercy would be a mark of great spiritual maturity. It would fuse hermeneutic logic with our yearning to mimic the Divine. For Elimelekh, the goal of Torah interpretation is therefore understood to be the increase of compassion. Or, to put it another way, only one who has internalized the thirteen attributes of God's compassion is fit to nuance Rabbi Ishmael's principles of Torah interpretation (*Yesod Ha'avodah,* 10).

2

Verses of Song

פסוקי דזמרה

P'sukei D'zimrah

2.1 The Hidden God

הִסְתַּרְתָּ פָנֶיךָ הָיִיתִי נִבְהָל

WHEN YOU HID YOUR FACE, I WAS TERRIFIED. (Psalm 30:8)

With this phrase from Psalm 30:8, *Nusach Sefarad,* the Sephardi rite, begins the *Pesukei D'zimrah.* It evokes the phrase in Deuteronomy 31:18 where God says, "I WILL SURELY HIDE MY FACE...." The Hebrew employs a common biblical construction for emphasis by using two forms of the *same* verb, "*HASTEIR ASTIR.*" In English, this double verb is customarily rendered as "surely hide." But this repetition might also imply that there are two kinds of hiding going on. The first is that God is hiding, and therefore life seems hard or painful or even worse. The second kind of hiding is that the hiddenness itself is concealed from us. The hiding is itself hidden. We don't even know, in other words, that God is hiding. And that is the source of our terror and dismay! This is because we are more frightened by the fact that we don't realize that God is hiding (*Siddur Baal Shem Tov,* p. 71).

The first kind of hiding is tolerable. We remain convinced that even though we don't understand what's going on, even though God's face, as it were, seems concealed from us, still we remain convinced of God's presence. Indeed, if we understand that God is present but only hidden, that the hiddenness, in other words, has a purpose, then our present sadness is mitigated. But when the hiddenness is itself concealed, then the terror of meaninglessness overwhelms us. Our goal, therefore, is a faith in and an abiding trust that the world is working out the way it's supposed to. And we are summoned to find the hidden meaning we trust is already there.

We have a similar teaching in the name of Dov Baer of Mezritch: Once Rabbi Dov Baer was walking on the street accompanied by his disciples and saw a little girl hiding in an alcove, weeping.

"Why are you crying, little girl?" asked the rabbi.

"I was playing hide-and-seek with my friends," replied the girl, "but they didn't come looking for me!"

Rabbi Dov Baer sighed and said to his students, "In the answer and the tears of that little girl I heard the weeping of the *Shekhinah*, '… And I will surely hide My face …' (Deut. 31:18). I, God, have hidden Myself too, as it were, but no one comes to look for Me!'" (*Itturay Torah*, ed. Aaron Jacob Greenberg [Jerusalem: Yahneh, 1987], vol. 6, pp. 198–99).

2.2 Decrees

בָּרוּךְ גּוֹזֵר וּמְקַיֵּם

Blessed is the One who sustains by decreeing.

The Hebrew literally says, *gozer um'kayem*, "the One who decrees and fulfills" or "the One who decrees and causes [the decree] to endure."

In Rabbinic Hebrew the word *gozer*, "decree," has a harsh, even punitive connotation. In the Yom Kippur liturgy, for example, we ask God to "avert the stern *decree*," or we speak in Hebrew of an anti-Semitic edict or persecution using the same verbal root, *gozer!* It is surprising therefore, notes Abraham Jacob Friedmann, the Sadagora Rebbe (1819–1883), that this morning prayer should begin by using a word with such bitter connotations and then—to make matters even worse—to follow it immediately by requesting inflexibility, "… and causes [the decree] to endure"!

Perhaps the solution depends on how we read the second word, *um'kayem*, "and causes [the decree] to endure." Perhaps the referent here is *not* the decree but the worshiper! Yes, the business of living is often inescapably contorted by one "stern decree" after another; from that there is simply no escape. The question is, can we make it through the pain of the present moment and survive? Can we endure? Whenever we receive a harsh life decree, suggests the Sadagora Rebbe, God simultaneously also gives *us* the power to prevail over it and to endure.

The Hasidim of Eliezer Zusya Portugal, the Skulener Rebbe, imprisoned by the Communist Romanian government for his religious teaching and efforts on behalf of Jewish children, tell the story of how he arrived at this same insight independently. Put into solitary confinement, he was compelled to find some way to maintain his sanity and spiritual compass. He devised a daily liturgical regimen. Each morning he would recite the service by focusing on each individual phrase, one phrase at a time. He would not permit himself to move on to the next phrase in the prayer until he felt he had found some personal message of hope and redemption. The result, not surprisingly, even for a mind of such enormous creativity and imagination, was that the morning service lasted throughout the entire day. And during his prayers, he too came to the identical insight that, while God might impose difficult decrees on us, God also grants us the spiritual stamina and resilience to endure and prevail. The Skulener's Hasidim recount that soon after attaining this insight, their rebbe was freed from prison and returned to his community.

2.3 Tears of God

SPLENDOR AND HONOR ARE BEFORE GOD; MIGHT AND JOY ARE IN GOD'S ABODE. (1 Chronicles 16:27)

In tractate Hagigah 5b, we have a discussion of sadness and joy in the divine precincts. The Talmud points to a verse in Jeremiah 13 that speaks of God weeping in a secret chamber. Rav Papa then points to our verse in Chronicles, "… MIGHT AND JOY ARE IN GOD'S ABODE!" which seems to disagree with the passage in Jeremiah. This apparent contradiction is then resolved when we realize that Jeremiah's weeping refers to the outer chambers, while Chronicle's joy refers to the inner chambers. In other words, in the innermost divine chamber there is always joy. In this way presumably God can respond anthropopathically to the human condition without compromising an innermost divine joy. One can also easily understand how Hasidism, with its emphasis on joy, would find this teaching so attractive.

It is significant therefore that Rabbi Kalonymus Kalmish Shapiro of Piaseczno, who ministered in the Warsaw Ghetto and may have been the last Hasidic Polish rebbe to preach on Polish soil, inverted our verse yet again. Read from within such a dark time, the Piaseczner understood that "… in God's inner chambers, God grieves and weeps for the sufferings of Israel.... God is to be found in God's inner chambers weeping ..." (Nehemia Polen, *The Holy Fire* [Northvale, NJ: Jason Aronson, 1994], pp. 199ff., 141).

2.♦ Serving in Joy

עִבְדוּ אֶת יְיָ בְּשִׂמְחָה
בֹּאוּ לְפָנָיו בִּרְנָנָה

SERVE ADONAI IN JOY; COME BEFORE GOD IN HAPPINESS.
(Psalm 100:2)

The Hebrew for "in joy" is *b'simchah.* And its prefix, *bet,* here translated as "in," can also be understood in this context to mean "through." Thus, *b'simchah* could mean either "in joy" or "through joy." Both offer sound spiritual advice. To "serve God *in* happiness" suggests that one should be joyous while serving God. According to the Baal Shem Tov and subsequent Hasidism, however, joy is more than merely an ideal state in which to perform religious acts. The joy itself becomes a necessary ingredient for all religious life, a primary religious category.

In the same way, sadness is also dangerous, for it is a confabulation of our evil side. When you are depressed, you are not only unhappy, your will is weakened, you are unable to act. You have literally lost the good fight. It is not surprising then that the second verse of Psalm 100 should attract the attention of Jewish spiritual teachers.

Sometimes your evil side leads you astray, convincing you that you have committed a grave sin when, in fact, you have done nothing seriously wrong or you may not even have sinned at all! The goal of the evil side is precisely this paralysis that results from sadness and depression. When you are sad, you quit serving your Creator. You must therefore be alert to such (self) deception of your evil side and say to (that "other" side of) yourself: "With your trickery and chicanery you want me to stop serving God, but I will have none of it!"

Indeed, even if you *had* committed a minor sin, you should remember that God draws great pleasure from your joy. And the ultimate goal, even more than your own perfection, is to please God. Preoccupation with religious failures, mistakes, and sins only debilitates a person, rendering him or her incapable of serving and pleasing God. Only when your tears are "tears of joy" is weeping acceptable. Beware of sadness; in the words of our psalm, serve God through joy (*Tsava'at Harivash,* 44, 45; 103:72; *Or Haemet* 102:2).

2.5 The Eternal Name

יְיָ שִׁמְךָ לְעוֹלָם יְיָ זִכְרְךָ לְדֹר־וָדֹר

ADONAI, YOUR NAME IS ETERNAL; ADONAI,
YOUR RENOWN IS THROUGHOUT EVERY GENERATION.
(Psalm 135:13)

In biblical Hebrew, *l'olam* means "eternal" (as translated here). But in Rabbinic Hebrew, *l'olam* can be understood literally to mean "for the world." Noting this, Zev Wolf of Zhitomir (d. 1800) in his *Or Hame'ir,* citing the Baal Shem Tov, asks the question: Why does the psalmist say, "God, your name is *for* the world"?

In order to appreciate his answer, we must remember that this four-letter divine name, the tetragrammaton, probably originally meant something like "the One who brings into being all that is." It is made from the root letters of the Hebrew verb "to be" and, like all names, mysteriously contains something of the inner nature of the one who bears it. For this reason, we must be especially careful, warns Zev Wolf of Zhitomir, not to confuse the essential nature of God with any name, even if it is the *shem havayah* itself, "the name of being." For even this most intimate, awesome, and essential of all God's names, which nourishes and vitalizes all creation, is nevertheless only an instrument of God's creative process. As we read in *Petach Eliyahu*, which begins *Tikkunei Hazohar* (a companion to the *Zohar* written in fourteenth-century Spain), "God, when You withdraw Yourself from them, even your names become hollow!"

Perhaps the *real* meaning of our verse therefore is, "Adonai, your name is only for *this* world (and those of us who dwell there), but your true God-ness is even beyond *all* your Names" (Zev Wolf of Zhitomir, *Or Hame'ir, Shoftim*).

2.6 Generations

דּוֹר לְדוֹר יְשַׁבַּח מַעֲשֶׂיךָ
וּגְבוּרֹתֶיךָ יַגִּידוּ

ONE GENERATION SHALL PRAISE YOUR WORKS TO ANOTHER;
AND THEY SHALL DECLARE YOUR MIGHTY ACTS.
(Psalm 145:4)

According to the *Noam Elimelekh* of Rabbi Elimelekh of Lizhensk, each new spiritual level is called a "generation." And in order to ascend to the next level above, you must learn to sanctify the ordinary, physical deeds of your present level. In this way, our verse from Psalm 145 now means that our daily actions like eating and bathing must also become expressions of praising God. We thus expand our spiritual reach to encompass ever-increasing spheres of otherwise mundane activity. One by one they too are now revealed to be instruments of praise.

2.7 Those Who Fall

סוֹמֵךְ יְיָ לְכָל־הַנֹּפְלִים
וְזוֹקֵף לְכָל־הַכְּפוּפִים

*ADONAI SUPPORTS THOSE WHO FALL AND RAISES UP
ALL THOSE WHO ARE BOWED DOWN.* (Psalm 145:14)

We have a tradition in the name of Rabbi Mordecai Yosef
Liener of Izbica commenting on the meaning of "sup-
porting those who fall." He teaches that not only does
God support those who fall (*somekh noflim*), but so must
lovers also. The Izbicer notes that according to Jewish law,
all you need to get married is a coin. But then why does
everyone use a wedding ring instead? This may be explained by considering the shape of a ring. It is round,
just like the Hebrew letter *samekh,* the first letter of the
phrase, *somekh noflim,* "Adonai supports all who fall...."
This reminds lovers that they must uphold one another
when they stumble or fall. They say, "With this ring," if
you fall, I will *samakh* you, I will support and uphold you.
You are not giving a ring, you are giving a *samekh.* Indeed,
when couples exchange rings, they pledge themselves to
be present to support and uphold one another. And surely
that is God's presence.

2.8 God's Majesty

כִּי־נִשְׂגָּב שְׁמוֹ לְבַדּוֹ
הוֹדוֹ עַל־אֶרֶץ וְשָׁמָיִם

FOR GOD'S NAME ALONE IS EXALTED;
GOD'S MAJESTY IS ON EARTH AND IN THE HEAVENS.
(Psalm 148:13)

Levi Yitzchak of Berditchev (1740–1810) in his *Kedushat Levi* (Jerusalem, 1958) draws a teaching from Genesis 2:4, "THESE ARE THE GENERATIONS OF THE HEAVENS AND THE EARTH WHEN THEY WERE CREATED—ON THE DAY ADONAI, GOD, MADE EARTH AND HEAVEN." He notes that when God created the universe, God made the heavens first, but as we learn from the reversed order of the end of the verse, this is not our goal. This same order of earth followed by heaven in Psalm 148 teaches us that the earth must come first. Our responsibility is to realize, that is, *make real,* the divine potential in the ordinary, physical reality of *this* world. Any beginning student of religion can easily see how to find God's majesty in the heavens and make them holy, but can we do the same for our everyday, mundane reality?

2.9 Every Soul

כֹּל הַנְּשָׁמָה תְּהַלֵּל יָהּ הַלְלוּיָהּ

LET EVERY SOUL PRAISE GOD, HALLELUJAH.
(Psalm 150:6)

The Hebrew word for "breath," *neshamah,* can also mean "soul." Levi Yitzchak of Berditchev, in his *Kedushat Levi* (Rosh Hashanah, Jerusalem, 1958, p. 277) understands "soul" as if it were a breath, a vapor whose natural state is floating upward. He reminds us, therefore, that at every moment our souls effectively want to leave us. Or to put it in a more sobering but accurate way, being alive is *not* the default position. The natural state of life is death. Without some intervening force, our souls would leave us all. It's almost as if what keeps us alive is that God, as it were, is pressing down on the lid and keeping our soul from escaping from our bodies into the void! Here we have an expression of core spirituality. Every moment is now worthy of the simple ecstasy of and gratitude for simply being alive. "Oh, I'm alive *again!* Yet another moment of life!"

To this insight, Rabbi Israel Friedmann of Rizhyn (1797–1850) adds another teaching. If each moment God literally restores our life anew, then, in addition to joy and gratitude, we should also draw courage when we pray. For often when we try to raise ourselves in worship, our *yetzer*, our self-destructive side, our own personal internal enemy, seeks to undermine our resolve by asking, Who are we to pray? How dare such a sinner open his or her mouth!

We must realize, says the Rizhyner, that each and every moment we are new creatures. Just this instant, again, we have been born anew. And therefore we are without sin!

2.10 Song at the Sea

אָז יָשִׁיר מֹשֶׁה וּבְנֵי יִשְׂרָאֵל
אֶת הַשִּׁירָה הַזֹּאת לַיי

*THEN MOSES AND THE CHILDREN OF ISRAEL SANG
UNTO ADONAI THIS SONG.* (Exodus 15:1)

The splitting of the sea happened twice! We have a second
tradition of a "miraculous splitting of waters" and Israel
passing through on dry ground, but few people think of
it when asked to envision the splitting of the waters. The
scene is recounted in Joshua 3:16–17, where we read that
"THE WATERS COMING DOWN FROM UPSTREAM PILED UP IN A
SINGLE HEAP A GREAT WAY OFF.... SO THE PEOPLE CROSSED
NEAR JERICHO. THE PRIESTS WHO BORE THE ARK OF ADONAI'S
COVENANT STOOD ON DRY LAND EXACTLY IN THE MIDDLE OF
THE JORDAN, WHILE ALL ISRAEL CROSSED OVER ON DRY LAND,
UNTIL THE ENTIRE NATION HAD FINISHED CROSSING THE
JORDAN."

Yet only the miracle of the splitting of the Red Sea
endures in the memory of the people. It is because of this
song they sang there. The miracle of the splitting of
the Jordan has not survived because there was no song
(A. Chayn, *Itturay Torah,* ed. Aaron Jacob Greenberg
[Jerusalem: Yavneh, 1987], vol. 3, p. 124).

2.11 Remnant of a Melody

רִבּוֹן כָּל הַמַּעֲשִׂים,
הַבּוֹחֵר בְּשִׁירֵי זִמְרָה

Adonai of all deeds, who chooses melodious songs.

Zev Wolf of Zhitomir, in his *Or Hame'ir* (*Yesod Ha'avodah*, 28), is struck by the pleonasm of "melodious" and "songs" used together. Either word would have sufficed. He solves the problem by suggesting that the consonants that make up *shir*, the word for "song" *(shin, yod, resh)*, might also be pronounced as *sh'yar*, meaning "leftover" (plural, *sh'yarim*, or, popularly, *shirayim*). Among Hasidim, *shirayim*, or "leftovers," refer to the crumbs remaining from a rebbe's meal. Though it strikes the modern reader as strange, to partake of these remnants—after they had been on the plate of such a holy person—was a great honor, even a gift. Disciples were known to fight with one another over the *shirayim:* the crumbs (or the songs!) from the master's table. It was not uncommon, furthermore, for each rebbe to have his (or her) own, either self-composed or favorite, melody. In this context, "melodious songs" now means "melodious leftovers" or "the remnants of a melody."

What remains when the music stops? Surely there must be more than dumb silence. The silence of the walk to the car after a symphony concert is now silent in a new way. The air is redolent with the remnants of the music. Some things simply cannot be uttered. And this is what God chooses: these remnants of song.

3

The Shema and Its Blessings

שמע וברכותיה

Shema U'virkhoteha

3.1 Blessing

בָּרְכוּ אֶת יְיָ הַמְבֹרָךְ

Let us bless Adonai, the One who is to be blessed.

The core rubric of all Jewish liturgy is the *b'rakhah*, the "blessing." The worship service itself is an elaborate sequence of blessings, one after another. It is only fitting therefore that the first words of the service summon us to blessing: *Bar'khu et Adonai*, "Let us bless God." But the word "blessing," perhaps as much in English as in Hebrew, is overdetermined, overused, desensitized, hollow. It sounds solicitous and connotes manipulation: "You're so nice. Please do us a favor." But according to Hayyim of Volozhyn (1749–1821), a kabbalist and possibly even a crypto-Hasid, "blessing" has a different primary meaning. In his *Nefesh Hachayim* (2, ch. 2), the Volozhyner cites the Talmud (Berakhot 7a) where Rabbi Ishmael is invited to actually pray *for* God:

"Rabbi Ishmael ben Elisha said: I once entered into the innermost part [of the Sanctuary] to offer incense and saw *Akathriel Yah*, Adonai of hosts, seated upon a high and exalted throne. God said to me, 'Ishmael, my son, bless Me!' I replied, 'May it be your will that your mercy may suppress your anger and your mercy may prevail over your other attributes, so that you may deal with your children according to the attribute of mercy and may, on their behalf, stop short of the limit of strict justice!' And God nodded to me...."

But how can a person actually bless God! Through speech, suggests Hayyim of Volozhyn, people can "call forth the divine flow of blessing." We can evoke what would otherwise have remained only latent, unrealized, unfulfilled. We cannot, to be sure, put something there that was not already there, but we can bring something into reality that was only hitherto a possibility. Thus the one who blesses becomes an agent of self-realization and fulfillment for the one who receives the blessing. We "conjure" a blessing. Even for God. And when we "bless" God, since God is the source of all life, we effectively enable the Holy One to bless us. In blessing God, we are blessing ourselves!

The one who offers a blessing is like a coach whispering to an athlete before the competition, "You can do it!" More than encouragement, positive spin, or sincere wish, the words of blessing literally bring forth and make real an otherwise unrealizable force. In this way, blessing is not supplication but symbiosis. God needs us to summon blessings, just as we could not live without them. And so the service begins: *Bar'khu et Adonai,* "Let us bless God...."

3.2 Light

יוֹצֵר אוֹר וּבוֹרֵא חֹשֶׁךְ

The One who forms light and creates darkness.

If God created the sun and moon and all the heavenly luminaries on the fourth day of creation, then where did the light that God created on the first day come from? The Talmud offers a daring solution, one with far-reaching implications for Jewish spirituality. Tractate Hagigah 12a suggests that the first light of creation was not optical but spiritual, a light so dazzling that in it Adam and Eve were able to see from one end of space to the other end of time:

"But was the light created on the first day? For, behold, it is written: AND GOD SET THEM [the sun and the moon] IN THE FIRMAMENT OF THE HEAVEN (Gen. 1:17), and it is [further] written: AND THERE WAS EVENING AND THERE WAS MORNING A FOURTH DAY (Gen. 1:19). This is [to be explained] according to Rabbi Eleazar. For Rabbi Eleazar said: The light that the Holy One created on the first day, one could see thereby from one end of the world to the other; but as soon as the Holy One beheld the generation of the Flood and the generation of the Tower of Babel, and saw that their actions were corrupt, God arose and hid it from them, for it is said: BUT FROM THE WICKED THEIR LIGHT IS WITHHELD (Job 38:15). And for whom did God reserve it? For the righteous in the time to come (cf. Avot

49

2:16), for it is said: AND GOD SAW THE LIGHT, THAT IT WAS GOOD (Gen. 1:4); and 'good' means only the righteous, for it is said: SAY OF THE RIGHTEOUS THAT THEY ARE GOOD (Isa. 3:10). As soon as God saw the light that God had reserved for the righteous, God rejoiced, for it is said: THE LIGHT OF THE RIGHTEOUS REJOICES (Prov. 13:9)."

The *Zohar* amplifies the legend.

"Rabbi Isaac said, 'The light created by God in the act of Creation flared from one end of the universe to the other and was hidden away, reserved for the righteous in the world that is coming, as it is written: "LIGHT IS SOWN FOR THE RIGHTEOUS" [Psalm 97:11]. Then the worlds will be fragrant, and all will be one. But until the world that is coming arrives, it is stored and hidden away.'

"Rabbi Judah responded, 'If the light were completely hidden, the world would not exist for even a moment! Rather, it is hidden and sown like a seed that gives birth to seeds and fruit. Thereby the world is sustained. Every single day, a ray of that light shines into the world, keeping everything alive; with that ray God feeds the world. And everywhere that Torah is studied at night one thread-thin ray appears from that hidden light and flows down upon those absorbed in her. Since the first day, the light has never been fully revealed, but it is vital to the world, renewing each day the act of Creation'" (Daniel Matt, *The Essential Kabbalah: The Heart of Jewish Mysticism* [San Francisco: Harper & Row, 1995], p. 90, citing *Zohar* 1:31b–32a; 2:148b–149a).

If the light of the first day of creation, that light of ultimate awareness, in other words, were to fall into the hands of the wicked, they would use it to destroy the world. (It's true. If we ourselves could see into the future, we'd make a terrible mess of things!) Yet, if God were to withdraw the light from creation entirely, deprive it of even the possibility of ultimate awareness, the universe would collapse, implode. So how did the Holy One solve the problem? God *hid* the light, but only for the righteous in the time to come.

Now if that be so, asks Elimelekh of Lizhensk (1717–1787), in his *Noam Elimelekh* (233, s.v. *re'eh*), why do we speak in the *Yotser* blessing, "Who forms light and creates darkness," in the *present* tense? We would expect the blessing to use the past tense, "Who *formed* light and *created* darkness." The explanation, he suggests, is that God—in an act of grace—is *continually* creating light. And thus, to the righteous the hidden light of creation, ultimate awareness, is revealed each and every day. It appears to them that, even as they are discovering light, God is continuously creating it for them. They feel as if they are actually growing into newly fashioned levels of awareness, each brighter than the one before.

As in so much of Hasidism, the vision here is not eschatological but psychological, deeply personal, and interior. The light is not a thing made in the past and hidden for the future but continuously created with each act of righteousness. In this way, the holy ones in each generation ascend into this hidden light, and the *Yotser* blessing invites us to join them.

3.3 Commandments

וְהָאֵר עֵינֵינוּ בְּתוֹרָתֶךָ
וְדַבֵּק לִבֵּנוּ בְּמִצְוֹתֶיךָ

And enlighten our eyes in your Torah
and may our hearts cleave to your commandments.

The second blessing prior to the *Shema* begins with *ahavah rabbah,* "great love." The primary symbol in Judaism for this love is, of course, our study of and devotion to God's Torah, the way of all creation. This yearning is expressed elegantly in a phrase in the middle of the paragraph: "May our eyes be enlightened with your Torah and may our hearts cleave to your commandments [*vidabek libenu b'mitzvotekha*]." The sequence begins with understanding, ascends through enlightenment, and culminates with cleaving to God's instruction.

In Hasidism, however, the word *dabek,* "cleave," means more than simply remaining close. *Dabek* has the same Hebrew root as the word *d'vekut,* arguably the goal and the fulfillment of Hasidic spirituality. Usually translated as "cleaving," "intimacy," or "staying attached to," *d'vekut* is nothing less than a fusion with God, a loss of self in the enveloping waters of the Divine, the *unio mystica,* a kind of amnesia in which we temporarily lose consciousness of where we end and begin, a merging with the Holy One(ness) of all being.

Rabbi Michel of Zloczow (1731–1786) explained that a person who experiences *d'vekut* loses all self-awareness and considers him- or herself to be nothing *(ayin)*, like a drop that has fallen into the sea and returned to its source, now one with the waters of the sea, no longer recognizable as a separate entity (Michel of Zloczow, as cited in Joseph Weiss, "Via Passiva in Early Hasidism," in *Studies in Eastern European Jewish Mysticism,* ed. David Goldstein [New York: Oxford University Press, 1985], p. 87).

Such a religious loss of self is also described by the contemporary American theologian Richard L. Rubenstein in an "oceanic" metaphor. He suggests that "God is the ocean and we are the waves. In some sense each wave has its moment in which it is distinguishable as a somewhat separate entity. Nevertheless, no wave is entirely distinct from the ocean which is its substantial ground" (Richard L. Rubenstein, *Morality and Eros* [New York: McGraw Hill, 1970], p. 186).

In this light we can understand how the phrase *vidabek libenu b'mitzvotekha,* "and may our hearts *cleave* to [or, unite with] your commandments," means more in Hasidic spirituality than a mere wish to live in accord with God's Torah. Through the observance of God's commandments, the worshiper prays to be rewarded with a loss of self, melding into the Divine, an experience of the ultimate unity.

Zev Wolf of Zhitomir (d. 1800), in his *Or Hame'ir* (*Ramzei, P'kudei,* 189) cites a passage in *Hovot Hal'vavot* (*Duties of the Heart,* by Bachya ibn Pakuda, c. 1080, Spain). There we read of a pious person who prayed that he be saved from *pizur hanefesh,* literally, "scattering of soul," becoming unfocused, fragmented, not being centered, "being all over the place." Such is the inescapable outcome of trying to own too many things in too many places all at the same time.

But Zev Wolf pushes the notion even further, suggesting that the main idea of having a "scattered soul" goes beyond being "scattered," to the sadness of having a "broken heart." (Psalm 34:19 speaks of a *"lev nishbar,"* a broken heart.) He teaches that the root of our depression is the "dis-unity" of our soul, our inability to be at one, our inability to serve the One God.

Now if you direct your heart toward constantly cleaving to God, then surely your heart would no longer be scattered or fragmented. The power of the cleaving to the One God would necessarily reunify your broken soul. The world may appear disorganized and broken into pieces, but in truth it conceals the Holy One, who sustains and unifies it continually. Everything in creation is but clothing for the Divine, which animates and nourishes it. It may, in other words, *seem* as if things are unrelated, contradictory, fragmented, "all over the place," but in truth everything is a manifestation of God and therefore the ultimate unity.

Martin Buber calls this "resolution." He teaches the same idea but focuses on the inner fragmentation that afflicts our souls. The person with a "divided, complicated, contradictory soul is not helpless: the core of his soul, the divine force in its depths, is capable of acting upon it, changing it, binding the conflicting forces together, amalgamating the diverging elements—is capable of unifying it" (*Hasidism and Modern Man, The Way of Man According to the Teaching of Hasidism,* ed. and trans. Maurice Friedman [Atlantic Highlands, NJ: Humanities Press International, 1988], p. 141).

So it is possible for the scattered soul to cleave to its Creator. And, since God's oneness is the root of all being, then to join oneself with God is to unify oneself. When you feel like you are drowning in a torrent of physical pleasures, dismayed by the multiplicity of your possessions and their demands, you return to the unity of God and heal yourself.

Thus, through Zev Wolf of Zhitomir's deliberate and creative "misreading" of *vidabek libenu*, "and may our hearts cleave," we are invited to consider that the source of our alienation from God's commandments, and even from God, lies in our personal disintegration, our fragmentation. In the *Shema*, which this blessing introduces, the reason we are unable to realize God's unity, and therefore the unity of all creation, is on account of our own brokenness. Before we can utter God's unity, then, we must recover our own. What more appropriate introduction to the *Shema*, the declaration of God's unity, could we hope to find?

3.4 Unity

שְׁמַע יִשְׂרָאֵל יְיָ אֱלֹהֵינוּ יְיָ אֶחָד
בָּרוּךְ שֵׁם כְּבוֹד מַלְכוּתוֹ לְעוֹלָם וָעֶד

LISTEN ISRAEL: ADONAI, OUR GOD, ADONAI IS ONE.
(Deuteronomy 6:4)
*Blessed be the name, the presence of its dominion
is ubiquitous and eternal.*

The theology of Shneur Zalman of Liadi, the Alter Rebbe of Lubavitch Hasidism (1745–1813), maintains that nothing exists but God. This "acosmism" denies the reality of the cosmos (hence: "a-cosmism"). God is not only the basis of reality, God is the *only* reality; God is all there is. Creation is continuously brought into being through the divine word. If our eyes could truly see reality, we would not see the material world but instead behold God's continuous utterance of the Hebrew letters, the real matrix of all being.

In such a radical monism, the *Shema,* the declaration of God's unity, means effectively that nothing exists besides God.

"'IN THE HEAVENS ABOVE AND ON THE EARTH BELOW, *EN OD*—THERE IS NOTHING ELSE [BESIDES GOD].' This means that even the material earth, which appears to the eyes of

56

all to be actually existing, is naught and complete nothingness in relation to the Holy One of Being."

As his editor explains in the English translation:

"The unity of God does not mean only that there are no other gods, but that there is nothing apart from God, i.e., there is no existence whatsoever apart from God's existence; the whole Creation is nullified within God as the rays of the sun within the orb of the sun. This is the meaning of *Yihudah Ilaah* (higher Unity)…" (Shneur Zalman of Liadi, *Likkutey Amarim* (Hebrew-English ed.) [London: *Kehot* Publication Society and Soncino Press Limited, 1973], *Shaar HaYihud v'Emunah,* chap. 7, 307–8).

But how do we reconcile the apparent contradiction between this acosmic vision and the inescapable experience of an obviously material world? Anyone can have a vision of the unity of all creation. It could be in a forest or by the shore of the sea. It could be during the concluding service of Yom Kippur or at the birth of a child. The question is, How do we bring the awareness of that higher unity into the everyday reality of *this* world? That is the challenge of sacred living: to realize more unity—with patience and devotion, to make *this* world resemble the one on High. And this is where Judaism parts company with the religions of the East. Judaism understands this yearning as a sacred obligation, a requirement for holy living, a commandment.

This is the problem that the Baal Hatanya, the author of the *Tanya,* teaches is solved with the second line of the *Shema,* which is a liturgical addition not found in the biblical text from which all the rest of the Shema is taken. He suggests that reciting this phrase is actually our attempt to bring the supernal unity spoken of in "LISTEN ISRAEL: ADONAI OUR GOD, ADONAI IS ONE" back into this world: *Barukh shem k'vod malkhuto l'olam va'ed,* "Blessed be the name, the presence of its dominion is ubiquitous and eternal."

"We may now understand," he suggests, "the statement in the holy *Zohar* [2:134a] that the verse *Shema yisrael* is *Yihudah Ilaah* ('higher Unity'), and *Barukh shem k'vod malkhuto l'olam va'ed* is *Yihudah Tataah* ('lower Unity')." The Baal Hatanya's editor goes on to explain that according to traditional rules of Hebrew grammar, the alphabet is divided into groups of letters, those in each group being interchangeable with one another. The letters *alef, hey, vav,* and *yod* fall into one group, permitting *alef* to be interchanged with *vav*. The letters *alef, het, hey,* and *ayin* fall into another group, permitting *het* to be interchanged with *ayin*. In this way *ehad (alef, het, dalet)* becomes *va'ed (vav, ayin, dalet)* (*Shaar HaYihud v'Emunah,* chap. 7, 307–8).

So the *ehad* of the *Shema* is the *Yihudah Ilaah* (higher Unity), seemingly unattainable in this world, only a dim memory of a sacred moment. But the *va'ed* of the *Barukh shem k'vod* is the *Yihudah Tataah* (lower Unity), our bringing the oneness of the Holy One into our daily lives.

Now we are ready to recite the *Shema* and its response.

3.5 Likeness

מִי כָמֹכָה בָּאֵלִם יְיָ
מִי כָּמֹכָה נֶאְדָּר בַּקֹּדֶשׁ
נוֹרָא תְהִלֹּת עֹשֵׂה פֶלֶא

WHO IS LIKE YOU AMONG THE GODS, ADONAI!
WHO IS LIKE YOU, WONDROUS IN HOLINESS,
AWESOME IN PRAISES, PERFORMING MIRACLES!
(Exodus 15:11)

Elimelekh of Grodzisk (d. 1892), in his *Divrei Elimelekh* (158), offers an extraordinary insight into the meaning of redemption. It is based on a deliberate misreading of the *Mi chamokhah* and a daring Zoharic interpretation of Adam and Eve's sin in the Garden of Eden. Elimelekh begins with a traditional reading: MI CHAMOKHAH BA'ELIM ADONAI, "WHO IS LIKE YOU AMONG THE GODS, ADONAI!" It is an exclamatory question: "God, You are incomparable, inconceivable, and incomprehensible. You are beyond any name or euphemism." In the words of the kabbalists, God is *Ayn Sof,* "the One without end," or *Ayin,* "Nothing." Nevertheless, as a concession to the needs of humanity and for our own good, God clothes Godself with qualities and names and actions, with *yesh,* "something." In this way we can know in a concrete manner how to serve and comprehend God.

People too need to maintain this balance between ayin, "nothing," and *yesh*, "something." In human terms, *ayin*, or nothingness, is egolessness, selflessness, radical humility. One needs to strip away all corporeality and all substance and be, in one's own eyes, simply nothing. But this also creates a religious problem, since radical humility or egolessness is also debilitating. How could one who is utterly nothing serve the Holy One of all being? How could an ant serve an eagle? Somehow, therefore, without losing our sense of nothingness, we must, at the same time, inflate ourselves with the notion that our actions, our service might actually be like sweet fragrances of the sacrificial altar in the Temple, ascending to God. Otherwise, there would be no need for human action. We must, in other words, through humility and selflessness be *ayin*, "nothing," while through our deeds and service strive also to be *yesh*, "something."

This also finds a kabbalistic parallel to the two trees in the Garden of Eden. The tree of life corresponds in mystical imagery to *Ayn Sof*, "the One without end," *Ayin*, "Nothing" (the top of the sefirotic diagram). The tree of knowledge of good and evil corresponds to this world of multiplicity, division, corporeality, and tangible reality— *yesh*, "something" (the bottom of the sefirotic diagram), the world of action. The goal is to balance the two trees. And that, says the *Zohar*—in a daring teaching—was the sin of Adam and Eve: They only "ate from the tree of knowledge but *not* from the tree of life!" The goal is to eat from *both* trees, to restore the balance between *ayin* and *yesh*, "nothing" and "something," and, in so doing, to repair the sin of Adam and Eve.

And just this is the real meaning of *MI CHAMOKHAH BA'ELIM ADONAI*, "WHO IS LIKE YOU AMONG THE GODS, ADONAI!" For the kabbalists, the word *mi* is not an interrogative

"who," but another name for God. And BA'ELIM, "AMONG
THE GODS" can also be read as *bet ilan,* "two trees." So now
it reads not as a question but as a statement: "Who [i.e.,
God] is two trees," the tree of life, which is *ayin,* "nothingness," and the tree of knowledge of good and evil, which
is *yesh,* "something," "… awesome in praises, performing
miracles!" And when we balance our power to act, our
self-assertion, our *yesh,* our something, with the humility
of being selfless, *ayin,* nothing, then we too can perform
wonders. And this is redemption.

3.6 Lying Down

הַשְׁכִּיבֵנוּ יְיָ אֱלֹהֵינוּ לְשָׁלוֹם
וְהַעֲמִידֵנוּ מַלְכֵּנוּ לְחַיִּים

*Let us to lie down, Adonai our God, in peace
and awaken us, O God, to life.*

According to an old midrashic tradition, recounted by
Rabbi Abraham ben David and cited in *Siddur Hahidah*
by Rabbi Hayim Yosef David Azulai, the origins of the
Hashkiveinu date all the way back to the first watch-night
in Egypt. That was when God warned the people of Israel
to remain indoors for their own protection. This was
because once the "destroyer" was let loose on the
Egyptians, he would no longer be able to discern between
who was deserving of punishment and who was innocent.
God said, in effect, "This is something I must do but must
not." Our only protection, therefore, was to stay at home.
And the memory of that ancient, archaic horror, suggests
Avram ben David, made an indelible imprint on our psyches, inspiring the first lines of this blessing: "Let us to lie
down, Adonai our God, in peace, and awaken us, O God,
to life"—safe from the terrors of the night.

3.7 The Adversary

וְהָסֵר שָׂטָן מִלְּפָנֵינוּ וּמֵאַחֲרֵינוּ

And remove the adversary from before and from after us.

Siddur Helkat Yehoshua by Rabbi Yechiel Yehoshua, the Biala Rebbe, recounts a teaching that the author attributes to his mother. Instead of reading the sentence in its apparent and literal spatial sense of "before" and "after," we should understand it temporally. Our adversary, our enemy, *hasatan,* assails us just before and just after we perform any religious deed. Before attempting to fulfill any mitzvah, we are challenged by an interior and psychic adversary who mocks us with the question, "And just who do you think you are to perform such a mitzvah? You are unworthy; you are unfit." In this way it seeks to debilitate us with doubt. And, should we have the temerity to try to serve God anyway, once we have completed the mitzvah, our interior adversary tries to destroy whatever good we might have accomplished by getting us to commit the even greater sin of prideful arrogance: "Look at me; I am so holy—I have just performed a holy act!" And that, the Biala rebbe's mother teaches, is the real adversary who is "before" us and "behind" us.

The Standing Prayer

עמידה

Amidah

4.1 Open My Lips

אֲדֹנָי שְׂפָתַי תִּפְתָּח וּפִי יַגִּיד תְּהִלָּתֶךָ

ADONAI, OPEN MY LIPS THAT MY MOUTH
MAY DECLARE YOUR PRAISE. (Psalm 51:17)

It seems odd that as a prelude to the *Amidah*—a bouquet of prayers of praise, petition, and thanksgiving, the most intensely conversational script of the entire siddur—someone thought to throw in Psalm 51:17: "ADONAI, OPEN MY LIPS SO THAT MY MOUTH MAY DECLARE YOUR PRAISE."

Wouldn't it make more sense to say something like, "Here I am God, ready to begin our conversation," or "Permit me to introduce myself," or "I know we haven't always seen eye to eye on certain things," something that would accentuate the dialogic nature of what will follow? For there to be a conversation, an intercession, there must be two discrete parties. It takes two to tango.

In much (but not all) of the Bible and the siddur, God and people are separate, distinct, discrete, autonomous, independent, and apart from one another. God says this, we say that. God does this, we do that. God's there, we're here. The energy of the whole thing comes precisely from our being separate from one another. So why begin our personal prayers with a denial of that mutual autonomy and free will?

The psalm says, "God, would you please open my mouth." Hey, who's working my mouth anyway, me or God? Who's praising God, me or God? What's going on here?

What's going on here is another spiritual paradigm, one in which God and people are not only *not* distinct from one another but are literally *within* one another. God is the ocean and we are the waves. In the words of the Hasidic maxim, *alts is Gott,* "It's all God." My mouth is God's mouth. My praises are God's words. In the teaching of Rabbi Kalonymus Kalmish Shapiro of Piaseczno (who perished in the Warsaw Ghetto), "Not only does God hear our prayers, God prays them through us as well!"

The words of the *Amidah* that will follow may *sound* like they come from me, but in truth they come from a higher source. Prayer may ultimately be an exercise for helping us let go of our egos, hopelessly anchored to this world where one person is discrete from another and from God, and soar to the heavens where we realize there is a holy One to all being and that we have been an expression of it all along. "ADONAI, OPEN MY LIPS THAT MY MOUTH MAY DECLARE YOUR PRAISE."

Rabbi Israel of Rizhyn, cited in *Yesod Ha'avodah,* asks: Why, now, at this point so far into the liturgy, are we asking God to open our lips? Would not such a request have made more sense at the beginning of worship? The reason, he explains, is that the liturgy is structured to correspond to what, in Lurianic Kabbalah, is called the four worlds. These four hierarchical orders of being are *atsilut* (emanation), *b'riah* (creation), *yetsirah* (formation), and, *asiyah* (doing). According to a model suggested by the kabbalist Moses Cordovero, they are often likened to stages in the creative process. First, there is *atsilut* (emanation), corresponding to inspiration, the germ of an idea. Following this comes *b'riah* (creation), corresponding to a vision of the finished product. Then we have *yetsirah* (formation), corresponding to the final blueprint, the musical score, the sketch, the instructions, the diagram. Finally, there is *asiyah* (doing), the finished artistic creation. Israel of Rizhyn suggests that the liturgy effectively begins from the bottom and swims upstream to its goal of *atsilut* (emanation). For this reason, the ultimate request that God open our lips must await the *Amidah,* or *atsilut.* With this total surrender, we lose the ability to voluntarily even open our mouths. There is no longer an "I," no longer one who can do anything. And so therefore we say, "ADONAI, OPEN MY LIPS SO THAT MY MOUTH MAY DECLARE YOUR PRAISE."

4.2 Abraham

בָּרוּךְ אַתָּה יְיָ מָגֵן אַבְרָהָם

Blessed are You, Adonai, protector of Abraham.

The *Amidah* is an anthology of blessings designed to walk us through a comprehensive spiritual regimen: parents, divine power, holiness, service, gratitude, peace. Much has been written about the importance of each theme and its place in the larger sequence, but Nosson Sternhartz, the amanuensis of Nachman of Breslov, in his *Likkutei Halakhot* (*Orach Hayim*, 1), asks, Why begin with parents, specifically Abraham? Could it perhaps be due to some particularly "prayerful" characteristic of the first Jewish father? And does the unconditional, selfless love of a parent teach us something about the nature of prayer itself?

We know that the patriarchs (and matriarchs), according to the Talmud (Berakhot 26b), established the three daily services: Abraham "AROSE EARLY" (Gen. 22:3), and so he initiated *Shacharit;* Isaac "WALKED IN THE AFTERNOON" (Gen. 24:63) and began the *Minchah* prayers; and Jacob "CAME UPON A PLACE AS THE SUN SET" (Gen. 28:11) and was the first to pray *Ma'ariv.* But this only raises a larger problem. How could our fathers and mothers have known how to pray if the Torah had not yet been given? The answer, suggests Rabbi Nosson, was that even before the Torah was revealed at Sinai, there was divine *hesed* or love,

70

which is the basis of Torah and therefore of creation itself. And our "parents," Abraham and Sarah and their children and grandchildren, were therefore able to "pray" directly through loving service. And the core of this "service" was *hesed hinam,* or "freely given love," love without any thought of return.

According to a similar tradition, not only was Abraham the first to begin to teach the world about the unity of God, he is the very foundation of the world. In Genesis 2:4 we read, "THESE ARE THE GENERATIONS OF THE HEAVENS AND THE EARTH, WHEN GOD CREATED THEM [*B'HIBARAM*]." And according to *Midrash Genesis Rabbah* 12:9, the Hebrew letters that make up *b'hibaram,* or "when God created them," can be rearranged to spell *b'Avraham,* or "with Abraham." In such a way Abraham and his service of "freely given love" are the very basis of creation itself!

Indeed, in Genesis 12:2, God blesses Abraham by saying, "BE A BLESSING." What this means, says Nosson, is not merely that Abraham will bless people, but that Abraham's name will be used to literally conclude the first blessing of the *Amidah,* "Blessed are You, Adonai, protector of *Abraham.*" So, this one, who knew of *hesed hinam,* "freely given love," *even before* the Torah and who was also the first to understand that there was only one God, is therefore the one in whose name we commence the *Amidah.* And when we, Abraham and Sarah's progeny, rise to recite the *Amidah,* our great-great-grandfather stands with us as we too invoke the source of all prayer: unconditional, freely given love.

4.3 Resurrection

בָּרוּךְ אַתָּה יְיָ מְחַיֵּה הַמֵּתִים

Blessed are You, Adonai, who gives life to the dead.

We have a tradition never to push away anyone no matter what he might have done or how far away she might have strayed (2 Sam. 14:14). Indeed, when we say that God's compassion extends to all creatures (Ps. 145:9), it means even to ones who seem to be hopelessly lost, spiritually dead. But how does this compassionate energy reach them?

According to one tradition (*Divrei Shmuel, Sha'arei Tefillah, Yesod Ha'avodah,* 36–37) the Hebrew letters are not merely signs for sounds but the very instruments through which the world comes into being. Words literally make reality; we create as we speak. (Some claim that "abracadabra" is an Aramaic contraction of *avara k'davara,* meaning, "I create as I speak!") And *Divrei Shmuel* suggests that similarly, when we pray, we are able to activate the creative divine power residing in the letters and words of the prayer.

In just this way, we are able to bring those who seem to be hopelessly lost, spiritually dead, "back to life." We begin with the purity of intention and focus on ourselves, then we shift our attention to the letters themselves, awakening the power latent within them, and finally, we

72

share this life-giving energy with "those who sleep in the dust." We become agents of the Divine in spreading God's life-giving power in and through the letters. "Blessed are You, Adonai, who gives life to the dead!"

4.4 Sanctification

קָדוֹשׁ קָדוֹשׁ קָדוֹשׁ יְיָ צְבָאוֹת
מְלֹא כָל הָאָרֶץ כְּבוֹדוֹ

HOLY, HOLY, HOLY, ADONAI OF HOSTS,
THE FULLNESS OF THE EARTH IS GOD'S PRESENCE.
(Isaiah 6:3)

According to *Keter N'hora,* associated with the circle of Levi Yitzchak of Berditchev (1740–1810), the recitation of "The Sanctification of God" (or the *Kedushah*) is to be accompanied by a meditative and bodily sacred choreography. We should, first of all, intend to fulfill the injunction "AND I [GOD] SHALL BE SANCTIFIED *AMONG* THE CHILDREN OF ISRAEL" (Lev. 22:32). And during the *hazarat hashatz* (the prayer leader's repetition), we should close our eyes. Everything in the blessing should be spoken quietly, except for the "HOLY, HOLY, HOLY" (*KADOSH, KADOSH, KADOSH*), which should be pronounced in a loud voice. And while you are doing so, you should look upward but with closed eyes!

We should also contemplate Isaiah 6:3, from which the prayer is taken, in its Aramaic translation (another version of the *Kedushah* called the *Kedushah D'sidra,* and recited near the conclusion of the morning service, actually contains this translation). From here we learn that the first "holy" refers to God's holiness in the heaven above, the residence of the Divine. The second "holy" is God's holiness on earth, the handiwork of divine creativity. And the third "holy" evokes God's holiness in time, for ever and ever. This then is the meaning of the next phrase in the Isaiah verse, "THE WHOLE WORLD IS FILLED WITH THE RADIANCE OF THE DIVINE GLORY!" God's holiness is heavenly, earthly, and temporal.

The Isaiah passage goes on to describe how the prophet saw a seraph (a fiery angel) "fly" with a pair of wings, "AND WITH TWO THE SERAPH WOULD FLY." Thus, through our own sacred choreography we literally "fly" just like the angels themselves! And this is the origin, suggests Rabbi Levi Yitzchak of Berditchev, of "fluttering" on one's feet, standing on our tiptoes with each mention of *kadosh*, "holy."

4.5 The Holy God

בָּרוּךְ אַתָּה יְיָ הָאֵל הַקָּדוֹשׁ

Blessed are You, Adonai, the holy God.

Rabbi Yehuda Aryeh Leib of Ger, author of the seminal *Sefat Emet* (1895, p. 165, *K'doshim*), suggests that there are not one but actually three modes of holiness. In *Leviticus Rabbah* (24:8), we learn, "Rabbi Abin observed that it is like a case wherein the citizens of a province made three crowns for the king. What did the king do? He placed one on his own head and two on the heads of his sons. Similarly, every day the celestial beings crown the Holy One of Being, with the three sanctities of 'Holy, holy, holy.' What does the Holy One do? God places one on God's own head and two on the head of Israel." But God's holiness is unlike ours. The commandment in Leviticus 19:2, "YOU SHALL BE HOLY, FOR I, ADONAI YOUR GOD, AM HOLY," might reasonably lead us to think that we are able to be *like* God. For this reason the text says, "I, ADONAI YOUR GOD, AM HOLY," meaning "My God-like holiness is utterly beyond your human-holiness."

We find this same idea echoed in 1 Samuel 2:2, "THERE IS NO HOLINESS LIKE GOD, FOR THERE IS NOTHING OTHER THAN YOU." Holiness is more than merely separating oneself from this world. For while God is beyond and separate from all creation (as it is written in Ps. 92:9, "YOU, GOD,

76

ARE ALWAYS BEYOND EVERYTHING"), God also creates every-thing and continuously gives it life—even while remain-ing utterly beyond and separate from it. And just this is the essence of the mystery of the divine holiness, for even though "THERE IS NOTHING OTHER THAN YOU," never-theless, You, God, sustain everything. For this reason, God is unique, remaining in a state of unattainable divine holiness.

And this also bears witness to the essential nature of God's holiness as we have it from Isaac Luria, where he talks about how God brought us out from Egypt. Luria notes that the Passover Haggadah says, "I and not an angel." (See also *Mekhilta, Pischa, 7.*) For not even an angel could survive entering the terrible defilement of Egypt. Only God, whose holiness is utterly beyond and "other" than this world in every way, could make it happen, as it says, "AND YOU [GOD] REMAIN EXALTED BEYOND EVERYTHING, FOREVER" (Ps. 92:9), meaning, "Even when You are in the world You are still exalted beyond it. "The psalm says, "*And* You ..." with a superfluous conjunction, "and," implying that the pious, or *tsadikim,* who become one with God, are also exalted and merit this quality of holiness. Even though they remain *in* the world, they are not *of* the world.

Like the *tsadikim,* Israel too has some of this quality of being in the world while also being beyond it. For this rea-son, Israel is above the angels. Even though the children of Israel went down into Egypt, nevertheless they were able to remain holy. And just this is what is hinted at in our midrash. While the angels are described as holy only once, Israel is called holy twice. Angelic holiness is ethereal, sep-arate, and distinct from the physical body. But another kind of holiness is bestowed upon Israel. Even though they have bodies and are clothed in physical form, nevertheless they are able to remain in a state of holiness!

And this is the meaning of "AND YOU SHALL *BE* HOLY," meaning that you must remain in your state of holiness, just as we read in Pesachim 23a, "in their being, they shall be...." Each Jew needs to guard that inner holy spark from becoming contaminated. As it is written in Psalm 101:3, "I WILL SET NO BASE THING BEFORE MY EYES; I HATE THE DOING OF THINGS CROOKED; IT SHALL NOT *CLEAVE* UNTO ME." We are to watch over ourselves, thereby fulfilling Leviticus 11:44 and 20:7, "YOU SHALL MAKE YOURSELVES HOLY," meaning that we will merit holiness and protect our souls from all contamination. This is the meaning of the praise that Song of Songs (2:2) bestows on Israel, "AS A LILY AMONG THE THORNS." Even though Israel is mixed up in this world, nevertheless it is like a tightly enfolded rose, whose innermost holiness is guarded always.

And this is why Isaiah 6:3 says, "HOLY, HOLY, HOLY, IS ADONAI OF HOSTS, THE WHOLE WORLD IS FULL OF GOD'S GLORY." This threefold repetition of "Holy" reflects a tripartite hierarchy of holiness! The first level of holiness is what we find with the angels: they are simply separated from anything physical. The second level of holiness is what we find with Israel: even though it is entangled with the physical world and frequently finds itself in impure situations, it nevertheless remains separate, distinct, and tightly enfolded. But God's holiness is even beyond these two. Even though "THE WHOLE WORLD IS FULL OF GOD'S GLORY," and even though God continually gives life to everything and brings everything into being, nevertheless—even though it is beyond human comprehension—God remains unique in God's holiness. God is in the world and *of* the world, yet *still* holy.

We could summarize the teaching thus: Angels are neither *in* nor *of* the world; they are utterly ethereal. That is how they remain holy. Israel is *in* the world but not entirely *of* it, as we were in Egypt. That is how we remain holy. God, in a way that is necessarily and logically incomprehensible to human beings, is totally *in* and *of* the world, yet nevertheless, still beyond it *and* holy!

And this is what our midrash is talking about when it speaks of our being holy like God. You might think that when it says "like Me," that it means that a person might be able to do whatever the heart desires and still remain in a state of holiness. Indeed this was precisely the perverse argument of the snake (Gen. 3:5) when the snake said, "AND YOU SHALL BE LIKE GOD, KNOWING GOOD AND EVIL." But God had warned us (Gen. 2:17), "ON THE DAY THAT YOU EAT FROM IT, YOU WILL SURELY DIE." For it was known to God that Adam and Eve were not permitted to be in such a state of heightened holiness. For this reason, the children of Israel need to continue to protect their holiness by observing the Torah's commandments, which describe both what we are able to do in holiness as well as those things that we must shun. If we do so, then the promise of our sages in Baba Batra 75b will at last come true. We shall be called "holy," just as God is called "holy."

4.6 Pleasures

כֻּלָּם יִשְׂבְּעוּ וְיִתְעַנְּגוּ מִטּוּבֶךָ

*They will be satisfied with and take pleasure
from your goodness.*

(Since it would be unseemly to make requests of God on a day that celebrates a complete and finished world, on the Sabbath the intermediate petitionary blessings of the *Amidah* are replaced with a special blessing for the holiness of the day itself.)

Aaron of Karlin, in his *Bet Aharon,* noting the apparent redundancy in the words "satisfied" and "take pleasure," reminds us that all desires and appetites, once sated, no longer provide much pleasure. But the pleasure of being close to God, he adds, is inexhaustible. Even though we will be satisfied, we will still draw pleasure from proximity to You.

ⴼ.7 Joy

יִשְׂמְחוּ בְמַלְכוּתְךָ שׁוֹמְרֵי שַׁבָּת
וְקוֹרְאֵי עֹנֶג

*Those who keep the Sabbath and call it a delight
will rejoice in your kingdom.*

Yaakov Yosef of Polnoye in his *Toldot Yakov Yosef* (s.v. *Ki Tavo*) mentions that his teacher, the Baal Shem Tov, wondered why it was so important to observe the Sabbath in ways so corporeal as eating and drinking. He answered his own question with a parable. There was once a prince who was sent to a distant, rural village where no one knew the royal ways or even of the king. In time, the prince became accepted as one of the locals. But then, after many years, he received a letter from his father, the king. He was overjoyed, but alas, there was no one among the townsfolk with whom he could share his happiness. These people had never heard of the king or of his regal ways. So the prince decided to throw a royal banquet at the inn and invite everyone in the town. There would be the finest food and drink for all. Even the simplest person could appreciate and share in such pleasures. It is the same way with our bodies, taught the BeShT: We must lovingly bring them along using pleasures they understand. Only then can we raise them to higher levels—corporeality enticed, sated, and ultimately raised to spirit.

4.8 Wisdom

אַתָּה חוֹנֵן לְאָדָם דַּעַת
וּמְלַמֵּד לֶאֱנוֹשׁ בִּינָה

In grace, You bestow wisdom on people;
to humanity, You grant understanding.

(With the blessing for wisdom, we return to the intermediate, petitionary blessings of the weekday *Amidah*.)

The *Degel Mahaneh Ephraim (Parashat Sh'mini)* of Rabbi
Moshe Chayim Ephraim of Sudilkov (1748–1800) cites a tradition from his grandfather, the Baal Shem Tov: Wisdom is
like water issuing forth from a wellspring. The more one
draws, the stronger the flow. And like life-sustaining water,
wisdom too increases with the space in which it can spread
out. In this way, when wisdom is allowed to flow into one's
personality and behavior, one becomes both physically and
spiritually purified. Such intellectual purification goes
beyond its source in the individual. Wisdom also nurtures
one's friends and students, even as they, by paying attention
and taking it into themselves, provide it with an ever-
growing expanse in which it can spread out and increase. For
this reason, this blessing should be understood as a request
that our wisdom flow forth—both within ourselves and our
circle of friends and students. One's wisdom only increases as
it flows forth and ultimately is given to others.

4.9 Repentance

וְהַחֲזִירֵנוּ בִּתְשׁוּבָה שְׁלֵמָה לְפָנֶיךָ

Bring us back to You in complete repentance.

In his *K'tonet Passim,* Yaakov Yosef of Polnoye (d. 1782), one of the Baal Shem Tov's principal disciples, cites Yoma 86b, which draws the famous distinction between *teshuvah mi'yirah,* "repentance motivated by fear," and *teshuvah me'ahavah,* "repentance motivated by love." Repentance from love not only makes expiation for the sin but actually, says the Talmud, transforms the sin into a merit! While the fact of the sin's having been committed remains unchanged, atonement transforms its meaning. Yaakov Yosef draws on what will become a primary tenet of Hasidic spirituality (and the reason Hasidism's opponents called it heretical): Since God's glory fills the whole world, everything is "full of the Divine,"—even sin!

Hemdah ("yearning, desire") is the source of all creative energy but also the source of all sin as well. With this in mind, Yaakov Yosef reminds us that there are two names for God. Before *hemdah,* or desire, gets us to act, God's name is the infinite and eternal *shem havayah,* that is, the four-letter *yod, hey, vav, hey,* but after we have acted and sinned from *hemdah,* God's name becomes *Adonai* (*alef, dalet, nun,* and *yod,* also spelled with four letters), which, according to tradition, implies divinity *in the physical* and all its inevitable limitations.

Employing *gematria,* the tradition of assigning numerical equivalents to each Hebrew letter according to its sequence in the alphabet, Yaakov Yosef goes on to suggest that the word for "sin," *chayt*—spelled *het* (the eighth letter), *tet* (the ninth), *alef* (the first)—may hint at the same insight. Together the two names of God—*yod, hey, vav, hey* and *alef, dalet, nun, yod*—have a total of eight letters, corresponding to the first letter of "sin," the *het* which is 8. The second letter of "sin" is *tet,* which is also the first letter of the word for "good," or *tov,* and has a numerical value of 9. Subtracting the *het* (8), which is the first letter of "sin," from *tet* (9), which is the first letter of "good" and the second letter of "sin," we are left with the last letter of "sin," *alef,* which has the numerical equivalent of 1, representing God.

Thus Yaakov Yosef concludes that even within each sin is a hint of the divine unity! And in a traditional Jewish universe, wherein letters are the building blocks of reality, his conclusions are compelling. While the logic of *gematria* may strike moderns as arcane, the conclusion is not only valid but even elegant: God is within everything, even sin!

When a person is aroused by *hemdah,* "yearning," he or she also arouses something in God. But if the yearning leads to the commission of a sin, there is a *kelipah,* or "shard," that effectively serves as a screen or barrier, preventing us from discerning the presence of God. Once one makes repentance *(teshuvah),* however, the screen falls away, enabling the penitent to see now the divine holiness "trapped" even in what was once a sin! In this way, through the process of *teshuvah,* or "return," one offers up all of oneself back to God.

4.10 Healing

רְפָאֵנוּ יְיָ וְנֵרָפֵא

Heal us, Adonai, and we shall be healed.

According to *Divrei Shmuel* (*Sha'arei Tefillah, Yesod Ha'avodah*, 37), the mother lode of all healing is *selichah*, "forgiveness." The business of prayer is not so much cure—that is for the physicians—but forgiving oneself, discovering acceptance, and thereby finding healing. When the blessing begins, "Heal us, Adonai, and we shall be healed," it is actually a request for a permanent change in the worshiper, that he or she not fall back into old patterns and habits. Each of our limbs (traditionally numbered at 248) will thus be increasingly nourished and draw its life force from the soul until there is no place devoid of holiness. Healing, then, is a psycho-spiritual state wherein we forgive ourselves and realize that holiness is everywhere, perhaps even in our own infirmity! Indeed, such forgiving acceptance may be a necessary prerequisite for all healing.

רְצֵה, יְיָ אֱלֹהֵינוּ
בְּעַמְּךָ יִשְׂרָאֵל וּבִתְפִלָּתָם

Find favor Adonai, our God, in your people Israel
and in their prayer.

Rabbi Kalonymus Kalmish Shapiro of Piaseczno, a modern Hasidic master who perished in the Holocaust, offers an extraordinary teaching about the nature of prayer in his *Derekh Hamelekh* (Tel Aviv, 1976, p. 93). He begins by citing Berakhot 7a, which asks the question: "How do we know God prays?" The answer comes from Isaiah 66:7, "I WILL BRING THEM TO MY HOLY MOUNTAIN. AND I WILL GLADDEN THEM IN THE HOUSE OF MY PRAYER": not "their prayer," but "my [God's] prayer."

We also have a tradition based on Genesis 28:11, normally rendered, "AND HE [JACOB] CAME UPON (*VAYIFGA*) THE PLACE (*MAKOM*) AND SPENT THE NIGHT THERE BECAUSE THE SUN HAD SET." We know from the way the word *vayifga* ("came upon") is used in Jeremiah 7:16 that it can also mean to pray (indeed, Berakhot 26b cites this verse as proof that Jacob initiated the evening *Amidah!*). And we further know that in rabbinic literature, the word *makom* ("place") can also mean God.

These substitutions yield three additional ways to

understand the verse: (1) Jacob prayed; (2) Jacob encountered God in his own act of prayer; and (3) Jacob encountered God in the midst of *God's* prayer! In this way, suggests the Piaseczner, God and Jew, as it were, pray together, finding one another in each other's prayers. The inner desire of the Jew is revealed as directed toward God, and the inner desire of God is revealed as being toward the worshiper. And in this way their mutual desire is united.

Prayer then is not so much an act of petition or a request for divine intercession as it is a gesture of uniting our will with God's. We say, in effect, I now want what God wants even as I discover that God wants what I want. The goal is not the granting of a petition but the moment of the encounter itself. In that moment, both our will and, as it were, God's will are united. We do not seek to nullify our will (simply nullifying your prayerful request or need would only be another way of reinforcing its importance); nor do we seek to alter God's will. We seek literally to unite our prayer and our will with God's. Thus, the innermost desire of the worshiper is revealed as a yearning to be with God, just as the innermost desire of God is to be with us. And this is the meaning of prayer.

Gratitude

מוֹדִים אֲנַחְנוּ לָךְ
שָׁאַתָּה הוּא יְיָ אֱלֹהֵינוּ

We gratefully acknowledge that You are our God.

Yaakov Yitzhak, the Hozeh ("Seer") of Lublin (d. 1815), reminds us of how easy it is to forget that everything issues from God—whether apparently ordinary or miraculous; whether through other human beings or directly from God, everything issues from heaven. And once we acknowledge this, once we understand how everything is therefore good, then it's ours forever. As we read in Psalm 136, "GIVE THANKS TO GOD, FOR IT IS GOOD, FOR GOD'S LOVE IS ETERNAL." If you acknowledge how good it is, then you can have it all the time.

Commenting on Deuteronomy 8:7, "FOR ADONAI YOUR GOD IS BRINGING YOU INTO A GOOD LAND, A LAND WITH STREAMS AND SPRINGS AND FOUNTAINS ISSUING FROM BOTH VALLEYS AND MOUNTAINS," the Hozeh goes on to explain that the water of the streams and springs and fountains is a metaphor for God's love and favor. And thus when we recognize how everything issues from God, then that divine kindness will be ours, not only in the valleys, when times are easy, but also on the mountains, even when life is difficult—all the time. The experience then of gratitude—and subsequent expression of thanksgiving—transforms everything into an enduring gift.

⌗.13 The Light of Face

בָּרְכֵנוּ אָבִינוּ כֻּלָּנוּ כְּאֶחָד בְּאוֹר פָּנֶיךָ

Bless us, our God, all of us, as one,
in the light of your face.

In his *Or Hame'ir* (Jerusalem, 1995, vol. 2, p. 305), Zev
Wolf of Zhitomir (d. 1800) is puzzled by how this blessing can ask God to bless all of us "as one." Surely the
needs of the aggregate community are many and diverse.
What one person lacks, for instance, another doesn't. How,
therefore, could this prayer institute language apparently
ignoring individual needs, lumping everyone together?
The answer, suggests Zev Wolf, is that each soul yearns
for God's beaming face, the *Or Hame'ir,* "the One who is
the source of all light." This is the reason that the prayer
states explicitly, "in the light of your face," denoting
God's presence. And in that pure, divine radiance there
is, of course, no differentiation whatsoever. There, everything is one. All individuality, all divisions, all differences
are absorbed.

It is only during the process of creation (Zev Wolf
understands this in kabbalistic terms as the seven lower
sefirot that construct the human personality) that the
"light" becomes differentiated into the diversity of the
world. Nevertheless, we intuit that the fulfillment of each
one of our individual needs can only be found in our

common, divine source. In this way we understand that each one of us can all be blessed "as one," with one blessing, by the Source of all the colors of the rainbow, which is itself beyond all colors. And just this is the mystery of peace: all the differences ultimately issue from a single source. "Bless us, our God, all of us, as one, in the light of your face."

5

The Reading
of Torah

קריאת התורה

K'riat HaTorah

5.1 The Ark

וַיְהִי בִּנְסֹעַ הָאָרֹן וַיֹּאמֶר מֹשֶׁה
קוּמָה יְיָ וְיָפֻצוּ אֹיְבֶיךָ

WHEN THE ARK WAS TO SET OUT, MOSES WOULD SAY:
ADVANCE, ADONAI! MAY YOUR ENEMIES BE SCATTERED. . . .
(Numbers 10:35)

The Torah reading does not fit naturally into the liturgy. Instead, it seems to be grafted disjunctively onto it from somewhere else. It is neither prayerful nor, like other biblical passages, woven into the flow of the prayers. It abruptly shifts the rhythm of worship from meditation, supplication, and thanksgiving into the study hall. What is going on here?

Perhaps the purpose of reading the Torah within the liturgy is not so much about hearing and studying the weekly lection as about something else entirely. Consider, for example, the following mystical traditions surrounding the scroll of the Torah itself. According to the *Zohar* (2:90a–b):

"Rabbi Eleazar taught: In these ten utterances [commandments] are embodied all the commandments in the Torah, decrees and punishments, cleanness and uncleanness, branches and roots, trees and plants, heaven and earth, sea and the depths. For the Torah is the name of the

Holy One. Just as the name of the Holy One is embodied in the ten utterances, so the Torah also is embodied in the ten utterances. These ten utterances are the name of the Holy One. And the whole Torah is one name, the actual holy name of the Holy One."

According to this, the commandments of the Torah are actually God's name. In the introduction to his commentary on the Torah, Rabbi Moses ben Nachman or the RaMBaN (d. 1270), the great thirteenth-century Spanish commentator and mystic, develops this theme:

"We have a tradition [subsequently alluded to in the *Zohar* 2:87a] that the Torah is composed entirely of divine names and that from another perspective the words separate themselves into names. Imagine, for example, that the spaces separating the first three words of the first verse in Genesis can be moved so as to spell an entirely different, yet equally true, statement.... And it is this way with the whole Torah...."

So, according to the RaMBaN, not only the commandments but the whole text is one long mystical name of God. Other kabbalists go even farther! Moshe Idel, of the Hebrew University, cites the kabbalistic text *The Book of [Divine] Unity,* which fuses the sign with what it signifies:

"All the letters of the Torah, by their shapes, combined and separated, swaddled letters, curved ones and crooked ones, superfluous and elliptic ones, minute and large ones, and inverted, the calligraphy of the letters, the open and closed pericopes and the ordered ones, all of them are the shape of God ... since if one letter is missing from the Scroll of the Torah, or one is superfluous ... that Scroll of the Torah is disqualified, since it has not in itself the shape of God" (Moshe Idel, "Infinities of Torah in Kabbalah," in *Midrash and Literature,* ed. Geoffrey H. Hartman and Sanford Budick [New Haven: Yale University Press, 1986], p. 145).

More than even God's name, the Torah here is understood as the shape of God. But the fourteenth-century kabbalist Menachem Recanati makes it explicit: "The letters [of God's name and of the Torah] are the mystical body of God, while God, in a manner of speaking, is the soul of the letters" (Gershom Scholem, *On the Kabbalah and Its Symbolism,* trans. Ralph Manheim [New York: Schocken, 1996], p. 44). The Torah, in other words, is more than the record of God's revelation. It is a manifestation of the presence of the Holy One, the shape of Divine—yes, even, as it were, "the body of God."

In this light we can now understand the passage from Numbers 10:35, chosen to accompany the procession of the Torah scroll through the congregation just prior to its reading. "WHEN THE ARK WAS TO SET OUT, MOSES WOULD SAY: ADVANCE, ADONAI! MAY YOUR ENEMIES BE SCATTERED, AND MAY YOUR FOE FLEE BEFORE YOU!"

In his commentary *B'er Mayim Chayim* (p. 48), Rabbi Chayim of Tchernovitz explains that the reason for the insertion of this verse at this place in the liturgy is that it is being used as a kind of battle cry against the forces of evil, or, as they are called in Lurianic Kabbalah, the *kelipot.* And the scroll of the Torah—a manifestation of, as it were, the presence of God—leads us in battle. Indeed, we realize that the main event may not be the reading but the actual march itself! In our procession with the scroll of the Torah, we are in effect carrying the physical presence of God out into the congregation and into the world! The great German talmudist Rabbi Jacob ben Moses Moellin (d. 1427), known also as the MaHaRil, goes even farther. He calculates the number of times the Torah is taken out and read before the congregation in one year—over 50 times on Shabbat morning, over 50 times during Shabbat *Minchah* (afternoon), over 50 times on Mondays and over 50 on Thursdays, 18 on Rosh Chodesh (the new moon), twice on Rosh Hashanah and twice on Yom Kippur, 9 festival readings, and so forth— and he comes up with a total of 248. And 248 is the traditional number of the body's limbs. Moellim concludes that this is because "everyone wants to see [God's] limbs!" (*Magen Avraham* to *Shulchan Arukh Orach Chayim* 134:2).

Something like this may also be in play with other rituals surrounding the public reading of Torah. Sephardim do *hagbahah* (the lifting of the open scroll for public inspection) *before* the actual reading itself, and in some Sephardi congregations, before the Torah is read, it is even carried through the congregation *open* in its case! Indeed, there is reason to conclude that the current practice of preaching and interpreting the Torah within the liturgy might better be saved for a separate occasion such as *s'udat sh'lishit,* the third Sabbath meal, as is the custom among the Hasidim.

5.2 Adonai, Adonai

יְיָ יְיָ אֵל רַחוּם וְחַנּוּן אֶרֶךְ אַפַּיִם
וְרַב־חֶסֶד וֶאֱמֶת

ADONAI, ADONAI IS A GOD LOVING AND GRACIOUS,
ABOUNDING IN KINDNESS AND TRUTH. (Exodus 34:6)

One of the core tenets of all spirituality is the paradoxical suspicion that, in the words of the late Professor Alexander Altmann, "God is in the self, but the self is not God," ("God and the Self in Jewish Mysticism," *Judaism* 3:2 [1954]). We sense the same divine Presence both in the world around us *and* within ourselves. Naturally then, when Moses ascends Sinai and gets as close to God as any human being has ever come, we might expect an insight into our soul's relationship with God. Indeed, as Moses is sheltered in a cleft of the rock while the divine Presence passes by, God proclaims, "ADONAI, ADONAI IS A GOD LOVING AND GRACIOUS...." In the liturgy for the Days of Awe, this passage appears prior to removing the Torah from the ark.

Noting the repetition of "Adonai," Levi Yitzchak ben Me'ir of Berditchev (d. 1810) offers the following insight into our relationship with God:

"The soul is a part of God. And therefore when the soul calls out to God in prayer, part of God is, as it were, calling out to Godself. So, when our text says that God passed by Moses' face, it means that Moses was overcome by reverence and filled with fear and love. And just this is the reason that the word "Adonai" is repeated. The first mentioning of "Adonai" is actually the aspect of God within Moses calling to its other, universal presence" (*Itturay Torah,* vol. 2, p. 268).

5.3 A Favorable Moment

וַאֲנִי תְפִלָּתִי לְךָ יְיָ עֵת רָצוֹן

AS FOR ME, MAY MY PRAYER COME TO YOU, O ADONAI,
AT A FAVORABLE MOMENT. (Psalm 69:14)

Yehuda Aryeh Leib of Ger, in his classic *Sefat Emet* (I "5635" and IV "5639"), deliberately misreads the supplication in our verse. The "favorable moment," he suggests, is not referring to a favorable time to *God* but rather a favorable time to the one who offers the prayer! And the best time, the most favorable time to pray for something, is when you already have it. The goal, in addition to wanting what you already have, is to experience what you already have now as a divine gift. Surely this would be a most favorable time to offer one's prayer!

5.4 Your Place

בְּרִיךְ שְׁמֵהּ דְּמָרֵא עָלְמָא
בְּרִיךְ כִּתְרָךְ וְאַתְרָךְ

Blessed is the name of the Master of the universe,
blessed is your crown and blessed is your place.
(Zohar 2:206a)

According to the *Zohar* (2:206a), we read:

"Rabbi Simeon said: When the scroll of the Torah is removed [from the ark] to be read to the congregation, the heavenly gates of mercy are opened and love is aroused in the world above. [Here] a person must say the following: 'Blessed is the name of the Master of the universe, blessed is your crown and blessed is your place. May your will be with your people Israel forever …'" (cf. *Wisdom of the Zohar,* 3:1037).

Opening the ark thus not only reveals the scroll of the Torah but effectively reveals the Divine. It makes God *physically* present. The words "your place" can be taken literally. God dwells, as it were, in the Torah. Drawing on this tradition, the Baal Shem Tov (*Siddur Baal Shem Tov,* p. 153, citing *Likkutei Dibburim,* vol. 2, col. 226) taught: "If [even] a simple, ordinary Jew, in faithful devotion and purity of heart, recites this Aramaic passage, 'Blessed is the name of the Master of the universe, blessed is your crown and blessed is your place. May your will be with your people Israel forever …,' God fulfills his request, if not all of it, then, at least in some respect, in part."

5.5 An Open Heart

יְהֵא רַעֲוָא קֳדָמָךְ
דְּתִתְפְּתַּח לִבָּאִי בְּאוֹרַיְתָא

Open my heart to the Torah. (Zohar 2:206a)

We read in Deuteronomy 10:16, "AND YOU SHALL CIRCUM-
CISE THE FORESKIN OF YOUR HEART." Commenting on this,
Rashi says that it refers to a kind of encapsulation or
obstruction of the heart and its covering. Puzzled by the
apparent redundancy of Rashi's mentioning both a "covering" and an "obstruction," the Baal Shem Tov explains it
thus: There are two kinds of spiritual impediments that
must be removed from the heart. One refers to the thick-
ening caused by sins. But this, in turn, creates a second
kind wherein a person, already desensitized by his or her
perverse behavior, now, in addition, refuses to even listen
to the chastisements and loving rebuke of friends. This
second form, suggests the BeShT, is what Rashi means by
"covering." Just this is the foreskin that must be cut away
in order for the heart to be open to holiness, and this is
why we pray, "Open my heart to the Torah" (*Sefer Baal
Shem Tov, Ekev,* p. 216, par. 29, s.v. *"u-maltem,"* from a letter by Barukh of Medzhibozh).

5.6 Cleaving

וְאַתֶּם הַדְּבֵקִים בַּיָי אֱלֹהֵיכֶם
חַיִּים כֻּלְּכֶם הַיּוֹם

AND YOU CLEAVE TO ADONAI YOUR GOD.
(Deuteronomy 4:4)

In classical Hasidic spirituality, the Hebrew verb *dalet, vet, kuf,* means not only to "cleave to," it connotes *being one with* God. This state of *d'vekut,* or *unio mystica,* is the ultimate goal, the fulfillment of religious living. It is not surprising, therefore, that Hasidic authors would pay very close attention to biblical phrases using this verbal root, as in this verse from Deuteronomy 4:4. Rabbi Menachem Mendl of Vitebsk, in his *P'ri Ha'aretz,* offers an extraordinary insight into this core yearning of human beings to be ever present within the Divine.

The main idea of cleaving to God, he suggests, is that there be no interposition, no barrier whatsoever, between the self and God. Only this absence of a barrier can enable the possibility of *d'vekut.* He offers a parable in the name of the Baal Shem Tov. It is impossible to glue two pieces of silver to one another without first "scraping off" or scouring the two surfaces; otherwise, there would be nothing to which the glue might adhere. Only then can fusion occur. He cites the verse from Isaiah 41:7, "THE

CARPENTER ENCOURAGES THE BLACKSMITH; HE SAYS OF THE
FUSION [PUNNING ON *DEVEK* AND *D'VEKUT*], 'IT IS GOOD.'"
Thus, they are made one. In the same way, if there is rust
or anything already on the surface of the metals to be
joined, then it will be impossible to glue them perma-
nently together. And this is the meaning of the verse in
Proverbs 2:4, "IF YOU SEEK IT AS YOU DO SILVER...." In the
same way, one who would cleave to God must also first
prepare his or her soul so that there be no trace of rust or
any other barrier that might be in the way. Only then will
the person at last be freed from grabbing onto other dis-
tractions and be able to cleave continually to God.

5.7 Giving Torah

אֲשֶׁר נָתַן לָנוּ תּוֹרַת אֱמֶת ...
בָּרוּךְ אַתָּה יְיָ, נוֹתֵן הַתּוֹרָה

Who gave us a Torah of truth ...
Blessed are You Adonai who gives us the Torah.

Zev Wolf of Zhitomir (*Or Hame'ir,* vol. 1, 8, col. 1) notices
the change in the opening Torah blessing from the past
tense, "who gave," to the present tense, "who gives." He
draws from this an insight into the nature of holy learning. The Torah *was given* at Mount Sinai. But in each
generation, God also *is giving* it anew through the new
interpretations of its teachers. The sages of each era thus
draw from sacred text newly appropriate readings for the
needs of every age. In this way, each "new" reading has
actually been secret and latent within the Torah ever
since it was first given at Sinai.

5.8 This Is the Torah

וְזֹאת הַתּוֹרָה אֲשֶׁר שָׂם מֹשֶׁה לִפְנֵי בְּנֵי יִשְׂרָאֵל

AND THIS IS THE TORAH THAT MOSES SET
BEFORE THE CHILDREN OF ISRAEL. (Deuteronomy 44:4)

Our sages (Yoma 72b) teach about this verse that if one is worthy, the Torah becomes an elixir, but if one is not, then it becomes a poison. This means, says *Sefer Hazichronot* (vol. 1, 345), that if one believes Torah is sacred, it gives life, but if one does not, it becomes toxic. But why should belief have anything to do with the purely intellectual business of learning a text, albeit a sacred one? Surely knowledge is simply a matter of getting something into one's head, whereas belief concerns matters that are beyond knowledge. Knowledge of Torah should therefore have nothing to do with belief (*Siddur Baal Shem Tov*, 157, 1st par.)!

In tractate Shabbat (88b), Raba says that the right hand is an elixir, whereas the left is a toxin. Rashi explains this to mean that the right hand devotes all its effort and energy to comprehending the secret meaning of sacred text. Thus, when one learns Torah, one needs to believe with a simple faith that each and every word conceals an inner secret. And one must therefore devote all one's mental faculties toward penetrating that innermost core. Such conviction purifies the learning of Torah.

To put it in a more modern idiom, when we confront a Torah text that initially strikes us as apparently self-contradictory, incomplete, unintelligible, or—God forbid—simply mistaken, we have only one of two options: "Either it is stupid, or I am." To say the former arrogantly seals us off from any further possibility of learning. To say with humility that there must be something more here that we don't understand opens the door to infinite learning. Indeed, long ago the *Zohar* noted that the stories in the Torah couldn't possibly be about what they seem to be about, otherwise we could write better stories (3:152a)!

In this way, the author of *Sefer Hazichronot* concludes that if we learn Torah with the humble faith that it must contain infinite mysteries and wisdom, we are purified through our study, and Torah becomes for us an elixir.

5.9 Open Your Hand

פּוֹתֵחַ אֶת יָדֶךָ וּמַשְׂבִּיעַ לְכָל חַי רָצוֹן

YOU OPEN YOUR HAND AND SATISFY THE DESIRE
OF EVERY LIVING THING. (Psalm 145:16)

Most of us are easily distracted into wanting specific
things that, we believe, will bring us happiness. In his
Kedushat Levi (vol. 2, p. 560), Levi Yitzchak ben Me'ir of
Berditchev (d. 1810) teaches that all of these cravings—
one specific thing after another—are only material man-
ifestations of God's love. Indeed, when we have God's
favor and grace, then we want nothing else. That free-
flowing divine love is the only real end of our otherwise
insatiable desire. Just this is the real meaning of God's
"openhandedness," and its fruit, the plenitude of divine
grace. Who could want more!

6

Supplication and Obligation

תחנון ועלינו

Tachanun v'Alenu

6.1 *Compassion*

וְהוּא רַחוּם יְכַפֵּר עָוֹן וְלֹא יַשְׁחִית

And God is compassionate,
forgiving sin, not punishing.

As its name suggests, *Tachanun* is a prayer of supplication. The traditional accompanying posture, known as *nefilat apayim* (literally, "falling on one's face"), involves resting one's head on one's arm. It is a gesture of abject humility before God's power and mercy, a gesture requiring the renunciation of any personal pride and all arrogance.

Michael Fishbane, in his *The Kiss of God* (Seattle: University of Washington, 1994, p. 107), notes that according to the *Zohar* (2:128b–129a) the recitation of the *Amidah* causes a coupling of the masculine and feminine dimensions of God. "In shame" before this "sefirotic" intercourse, the worshiper prostrates himself, covers his face, and focuses his thoughts on the birth of souls resulting from this holy union. "The purpose of this physical and mental exercise is to undergo a cycle of death and rebirth, insofar as the worshipper 'devotes his soul' to the feminine dimension. By thus cleaving to Her when She is 'taking' souls, the worshipper is born anew (*Zohar* 2:200b)." The "shame" felt here, concludes Fishbane, causes a spiritual transformation resulting from being one with God "during its process of regeneration" (107).

111

The ultimate expression of such humility is, of course, the willingness to die at the hands of the *Shekhinah,* the feminine dimension of God, symbolized by the tree of death. At the conclusion of the *Amidah,* during which the kabbalistic worshiper intends to be attached to the masculine dimension of God, the *sefirah Tiferet,* the tree of life, the worshiper, notes Fishbane, "must immediately acknowledge the feminine side of Death, that he not die altogether. 'It is thus necessary for a person—immediately upon concluding the *Amidah*—to regard himself as if (*ke'ilu*) he departed from the world' (*Zohar,* III, 120b). This is done through the mimetic act of *nefilat apayim,* whereby he falls face forward and (through reciting Psalm 25) redeposits his soul with the same feminine aspect of God with which he deposits it at night—but now not in a temporary way 'but as one who actually (*vada'i*) departs from the world' (*Zohar,* III, 121a)" (Fishbane, 108).

The contemporary teacher Rabbi Zalman Schachter-Shalomi, drawing on several mystical traditions, notes that the sequence of the rubrics of the liturgy correspond with an ascent through the four worlds of being and then a gentle return to earth. *Birkhot Hashachar* (the Morning Blessings) and *Korbanot* (description of the sacrificial rite), in their obvious physicality, correspond to *asiyah,* the world of making or doing. The *Pesukei D'zimrah* (verses of songs and praise) are much more emotional and thus correspond naturally with *yetsirah,* the world of formation and feeling. The *Shema U'virkhoteha* (*Shema* and Its Blessings), as expressions of belief and faith, correspond to *b'riah* (creation), which is understood in primarily intellectual terms. And the *Shemoneh Esreh* (the Eighteen Benedictions) or *Amidah* (the Standing Prayer) is the pinnacle of the liturgy. The worshiper is finally at his or her goal, alone with the One. In this almost orgiastic way, the *Amidah* corresponds to *atsilut* (emanation of the most ethereal). *Tachanun* (prayers of supplication) are what remains after the zenith of the *Amidah*. They are the *sh'ayrit ha'atsilut* (the remnants of ecstasy) or, as Schachter-Shalomi has suggested, afterplay. Finally, the *Ashre* (Psalm 144) and *U'VA-L'TSIYON* ("AND THERE SHALL COME TO ZION ...") in this schema are a form of *yeridat hashefa,* a drawing down of the divine radiance, making it one's own at the conclusion of the liturgy.

6.2 Reverence

כִּי עִמְּךָ הַסְּלִיחָה לְמַעַן תִּוָּרֵא

But with You there is forgiveness,
that You may be revered.

In his *Or Lashamayim* (1850), Rabbi Me'ir of Apta offers a comment on how the interdependence between God and the children of Israel can be used in a daringly creative way to secure divine lenience for our sins. He begins by citing Deuteronomy 28:10, "AND ALL THE PEOPLES OF THE EARTH SHALL SEE THAT ADONAI'S NAME IS PROCLAIMED OVER YOU [ISRAEL], AND THEY SHALL STAND IN FEAR OF YOU." Then he notes that Rabbi Eliezer teaches in Berakhot 6a (and several other places throughout the Talmud) that when this verse says "proclaimed over you," it is an allusion to *tefillah shel rosh,* the *tefillin* worn on the head. According to the Talmud, God too wears *tefillin.* But since it would make no sense for God's *tefillin* to have a piece of parchment proclaiming God's unity, the Rabbis imagine instead that they contain the phrase from 1 Chronicles 17:21, "WHO IS LIKE YOUR PEOPLE ISRAEL, A NATION UNIQUE ON EARTH." In other words, as Jews proclaim God's unity in the *tefillin* worn on their heads, so God proclaims the uniqueness of the Jews in the *tefillin* worn on God's head. But this also means that, God forbid, when the people of Israel defile themselves, they effectively defile the *tefillin* of the Master of the universe. Our flaw, our defect, disqualifies God's *tefillin*. And God, as it were, therefore has a vested interest in helping the people of Israel to be blameless. For this reason, when God hears our supplications and forgives our sins, God effectively repairs God's own *tefillin* and, as it were, restores the reverence due to God throughout the world. Just this is the meaning of the passage in the *Tachanun* prayer with which we began, "But with You there is forgiveness, that You may be revered." Now it means: For with You, O God, there is the capacity to forgive the sins of Israel, and only such reverence can repair God's *tefillin*.

6.3 Open Your Eyes

הַטֵּה, אֱלֹהַי אָזְנְךָ וּשְׁמָע
פְּקַח עֵינֶיךָ וּרְאֵה שׁוֹמְמֹתֵינוּ

My God, incline your ear and listen,
open your eyes and see our ruins.

Troubled and fascinated by such a direct anthropomor-
phism, Rabbi Levi Yitzchak of Berditchev (1740–1810) wonders how we could meaningfully speak of God as having
ears and eyes that could be open and closed (*Kedushat
Levi*, s.v. *M'tsora "v'Isha …"*). He finds a hint of the solution in Psalm 34:16, "THE EYES OF ADONAI ARE UPON THE
RIGHTEOUS; GOD'S EARS HEAR THEIR CRY." It's as if the psalm
were saying that the eyes of God originally belong to and,
so, come from the righteous, says Levi Yitzchak.

If, then, the eye sees something untoward, God forbid,
then that eye that is projected on High is effectively blinded;
by contrast, if the eye beholds something beautiful, then the
one on High is opened. And just this is the meaning of "My
God, incline your ear and listen, open your eyes and see."
When we pray that God, as it were, will hear and see, we are
actually alluding to our desire that we ourselves only hear and
see what we would regard as fit for the Holy One to hear and
see. Since our eyes and ears are at the same time God's, we ask
to hear and see only what we would want for heaven also.

6. ❦ *Support from Zion*

יִשְׁלַח עֶזְרְךָ מִקֹּדֶשׁ וּמִצִיוֹן יִסְעָדֶךָּ

*MAY GOD SEND YOU HELP FROM GOD'S HOLY ABODE
AND GIVE YOU SUPPORT FROM ZION. (Psalm 20:3)*

Rabbi Aaron of Karlin (d. 1872) in his *Bet Aharon,* offers
the following teaching based on Psalm 20:3, "MAY GOD
SEND YOU HELP FROM GOD'S HOLY ABODE AND GIVE YOU SUP-
PORT FROM ZION." He notices that the Hebrew word for
Zion, *tsiyon,* can be read not only as the name of a mountain and a poetic allusion to the Land and people of Israel,
but also as meaning "to make an impression or a sign." This
reminds him that the *tefillin* strap wrapped around our
forearm each weekday morning usually leaves a visible
indentation in the skin after it has been removed. This
impression, this sign, now literally on the skin of our arm,
thus continues to serve as a reminder and a support for us
long after the religious deed itself has been performed. In
this way, Rabbi Aaron of Karlin counsels, only if our religious deeds truly make an impression upon us can they
also be a source of support and nurture.

6.5 None Else

יְיָ הוּא הָאֱלֹהִים בַּשָּׁמַיִם מִמַּעַל
וְעַל הָאָרֶץ מִתָּחַת אֵין עוֹד

IT IS ADONAI WHO IS GOD IN THE HEAVENS
ABOVE AND ON THE EARTH BENEATH, THERE IS NONE ELSE.
(Deuteronomy 4:39)

The first of the two paragraphs of *Alenu* prays for a time when the Jewish people will lead all humanity to acknowledge God's sovereignty and exclusive reality. Each of the two concluding sentences ends with the thought that Adonai is our God and "there is none else." Indeed, the second sentence is a direct quotation from Deuteronomy 4:39, "YOU SHALL KNOW THIS DAY, AND REFLECT IN YOUR HEART, THAT IT IS ADONAI WHO IS GOD IN THE HEAVENS ABOVE AND ON THE EARTH BENEATH, THERE IS NONE ELSE." In each case, the plain meaning of the Hebrew is clear: our God is the only God. But Hasidic tradition, as taught by such masters as Dov Baer of Mezritch (1704–1772), Shneur Zalman of Liady (1747–1813), Yitzchak Isaac Epstein of Homel (1780–1857), hears something else.

The Hebrew is ambiguous. *Ayn od* literally means not just "there is *none* else," but "there is *nothing* else." This dramatically expands the theological assertion: Not only is God the only God, but God is also the only reality.

Besides God, there is literally *nothing* else; in the Yiddish, *Alles is Gott.* The technical term for such a radical monistic theology is acosmism, the denial of the reality of the cosmos. God is the substratum, the font of all being. If something is real, it can only be because it is a manifestation of the underlying and ultimate divine reality.

According to such a reading, the meaning of the *Alenu* shifts from a yearning merely that everyone acknowledge God's kingship. Now it becomes a yearning that all people see through the apparent brokenness, confusion, contradiction, and discord to the ultimate divine unity that is the true source of reality.

6.6 God's Will

יִתְגַּדַּל וְיִתְקַדַּשׁ שְׁמֵהּ רַבָּא
בְּעָלְמָא דִּי בְרָא כִרְעוּתֵהּ

*Magnified and sanctified be God's great name
in the world that God created according to God's will.*

The *Kaddish,* of course, makes no mention of death. But the *Kaddish* is all about death. It is about God's eternity and human finitude, and where they meet.

Dov Baer Ratner (1852–1917) speaks of this intersection in his commentary *Ahavat Tsiyon Virushalayim* on Talmud Yerushalmi (Yebamot 15:2). There the text cites Psalm 140:8, "YOU PROTECTED MY HEAD ON THE DAY OF ARMED BATTLE." The Hebrew for "armed battle" is *neshek,* which the Talmud notes can also be read as "kiss." The verse then becomes, "You protected my head on the day of the kiss." This, Ratner suggests, is the real occasion for God's promise of protection, the point where, as it were, the lips of one world meet those of another—for instance, "on the day the summer kisses the winter" (i.e., the autumnal equinox) or "when [one] exits this world and enters the world-to-come." Death itself holds no terror for the righteous, but the moment of transition from one world to another, the moment of the kiss—that is potentially a time of real danger.

Indeed, even for a great *tsadik*, who has served God throughout his or her entire life, the earthly world is, by nature, dark and impure when compared with the blinding radiance of the next world. When, then, a *tsadik* goes on to the next world of true light and life, the transition is disjunctive, even jarring, like the shock suffered by a newborn infant when it leaves the womb and is born into the bright light of this world.

Ratner suggests that the aphorism "The righteous are greater in death than in life" refers to this moment when this world kisses the next. The greatness of the righteous stems from their ability to make the transition, the jump, to the next world, with its overpowering burst of bright light, and somehow survive the leap. He concludes his teaching by citing the verse from Proverbs 31:25, which speaks of a righteous woman, "SHE LAUGHS AT THE LAST DAY."

6.7 The Messiah

אֲנִי מַאֲמִין בְּאֱמוּנָה שְׁלֵמָה
בְּבִיאַת הַמָשִׁיחַ

I believe with complete faith in the coming of the messiah.

The twelfth of Maimonides' Thirteen Principles of Faith echoes the first: from God to apotheosis. The beginning of faith is faith in God, and the end of faith is the hope that all flesh will be elevated, transformed into spirit. The symbol for this resolution of history, of course, is the messiah, whom only God can bring.

In much of the Jewish spiritual imagination, the time of the messiah is understood not so much as a radical change in the way things are, but in the way we understand them. The task requires increasing measures of stamina and dedication. Yaakov Yitzhak Horowitz of Lublin (*HaY'hudi Hakadosh*, the "Holy Yehudi"—*Nifla'ot Hay'hudi* [Jerusalem, 1987], 58b) teaches that the *tsadik*, a truly righteous person, must learn first how to make the world whole within his or her own self. But the more spiritually aware such a person becomes, the more he or she will realize the enormity of the task, until finally, the *tsadik* will comprehend his or her own personal similarity to the least religious and the most sinful. Indeed, when this happens to every person, the messiah's time will, at last, be a reality.

The Yehudi thus once explained the difference between the *tsadikim* (righteous ones) of any generation and the messiah. Of course, every *tsadik* spends each day in the service of God according to his or her level of attainment. And on the next day the *tsadik* adds to the preceding day's achievement. And so it goes, each day adding a little more. But with a *tsadik* who is the messiah it is different. He or she too must add a little more from the preceding day's accomplishments. Overnight, however, everything that has been achieved the preceding day is erased and taken away, so that on the next day the messiah must start all over again from the very beginning.

Spiritual wisdom is neither historical nor cumulative. Each person must begin from the beginning, start all over again, just like the messiah. It is not unlike the structure of the Thirteen Principles themselves. We must always begin with the nameless One, which we try to bring into ourselves.

6.8 None Like Our God

אֵין כֵּאלֹהֵינוּ אֵין כֵּאדוֹנֵינוּ
אֵין כְּמַלְכֵּנוּ אֵין כְּמוֹשִׁיעֵנוּ

*There is none like our God; there is none like our Master;
there is none like our King; there is none like our Savior.*

In his *Siddur Hahida,* Hayim Yosef David Azulai
(1724–1806) offers the following commentary on the repeat-
ing sequence of the four divine epithets in *Ayn Keloheinu.*

"*Eloheinu,* we have no God but You" refers to King
Nebuchadnezzar of Babylon, who, as recounted in the
Book of Daniel, told the Jews to bow down to an idol.

"*Adoneinu,* we have no master but You" refers to King
Ahasuerus, who, as recounted in the Book of Esther, sold
the Jews as slaves to Haman.

"*Malkeinu,* we have no king but You" refers to
Alexander the Great, who proclaimed himself the first
king of the entire world.

"*Moshi'einu,* we have no savior but You" refers to Esau
(a common poetic allusion to Rome and the Western
world), who claimed that there was another savior.

Thus, in each verse, the hymn rehearses Jewish history
and its travails, from Babylon, to Persia, to Greece, to Rome.
In each instance, then, this popular hymn becomes a pro-
found affirmation of Judaism's steadfast devotion to God.

7

The Sabbath

שבת

Shabbat

7.1 Sabbath Lights

לְהַדְלִיק נֵר שֶׁל שַׁבָּת

To kindle the light of Shabbat.

It is difficult to imagine a more primal ritual than the lighting of a candle. The simple mystery of a tiny flame—invisibly joined to a wick, bestowing light and continuously flickering upward—evokes a sense of the numinous in all spiritual traditions. The flame of a candle strikes us at once as a perfect metaphor for a soul (even one that has departed) yearning or, in the case of the Sabbath candles, renewed and reconnected to its source on high. On the Sabbath, each Jew, it is said, receives a *neshamah yetayrah,* an extra soul. And any Jew who has ever watched the Sabbath lights reflected in his or her mother's eyes knows this must be true.

Rabbi Levi Yitzchak of Berditchev, in his *Kedushat Levi* (*Hanukah,* second entry), reminds us that the Shabbat candles are indeed the first mitzvah of Shabbat—even before the *Kiddush* (or sanctification itself)—because once the candles are lit, the Sabbath has begun. And to light them, effectively, brings light down from above.

And, according to some, that light even obliterates the darkness of night: Rabbi Sh'lomo Leib of Lentchna once told his friend Rabbi Yitzchak of Vorki, after sharing a

Sabbath meal, that the reason we do not customarily say "Good evening" on Shabbos is that on Shabbos there is simply no darkness. And therefore, since there is neither night nor evening, it's all light.

7.2 Come, My Beloved

לְכָה דוֹדִי לִקְרַאת כַּלָּה
פְּנֵי שַׁבָּת נְקַבְּלָה

Come, my beloved to meet the bride,
let us welcome the presence of Shabbat.

L'khah Dodi, "Come, My Beloved," is perhaps the most beloved and widely sung Sabbath hymn of all time. It was composed by Sh'lomo Alkebets in sixteenth-century Safed amidst a cultural revolution that would come to be known as Lurianic Kabbalah. Mystical imagery pervaded every aspect of life. Professor Reuven Kimelman, in his *The Mystical Meaning of Lekhah Dodi and Kabbalat Shabbat* (Jerusalem: The Hebrew University Magnus Press, 2003), notes one of hundreds of examples in which the hymn operates on a concealed kabbalistic level.

Gematria is an ancient system of assigning a numerical equivalent to every Hebrew letter based on its sequential place in the alphabet. (It is the most popular, but by no means the only, system of extracting additional meaning from the letters and words of the holy language.) Thus *alef,* the first letter, is 1; *bet,* the second letter, is 2; *gimel,* the third letter, is 3; and so forth until we get to *yod,* which is 10. From then on, letters increase by tens until we reach *kuf,* which is 100. The increments now progress by hundreds until we reach the last letter, *tav,* which is 400.

Perhaps the single most commonly noted *gematria* is the numerical equivalent for the *shem ham'forash,* the ineffable name of God, the tetragrammaton: *yod, hey, vav,* and *hey.* The numeric value of God's most awesome name is thus: 10 + 5 + 6 + 5, totaling 26. And, while it strikes most moderns as arcane, it is difficult for even a beginning student of Kabbalah to encounter this number without pausing for a few moments of reflection. It is a very important number. Furthermore, kabbalistic tradition also understands the broken state of our present world to be manifest in the brokenness or division of God's name into its first two letters (*yod* and *hey,* i.e., 10 + 5 = 15) and its last two letters (*vav* and *hey,* i.e., 6 + 5 = 11). The messianic goal, then, would be to reunite the two broken halves and thereby bring them back to the ultimate total of 26.

This is all a roundabout way of understanding some of the extraordinary symbolism in Alkebets's hymn. The first half of the first line (*L'khah dodi likrat kalah*) has 15 Hebrew letters, and the last half (*p'nei Shabbat nikablah*) has 11, totaling 26, the divine name at last restored to unity!

7.3 Flame Fused to Wick

בַּמֶּה מַדְלִיקִין

With what may we kindle the Sabbath lamp?

Mystics have long been fascinated by the spectrum of light surrounding a burning wick. In one well-known passage, the *Zohar* explains the mystery of the colors of a burning flame:

"Come and see: Whoever desires to penetrate the wisdom of holy unification should contemplate the flame ascending from a glowing ember or a burning candle. The flame ascends only [51a] when grasped by coarse substance.

"Come and see! In a flame ascending are two lights: one, a white light, radiant; the other, a light tinged with black or blue. The white light is above, ascending unswervingly, while beneath it is the blue or black light, a throne for the white, which rests upon it, each embracing the other, becoming one" (*Zohar* I:50b–51a; *The Zohar: Pritzker Edition*, trans. Daniel C. Matt [Stanford, CA: Stanford University Press, 2004], 283–3).

Rabbi Isaiah Horowitz, cited in *Siddur Sha'ar haShamayim*, teaches that each lamp has its own deep mysteries. There are three colors of light corresponding to the *sefirot Malkhut*, the presence of God; *Tiferet*, harmony; and *Binah*, intuition. The dark blue flame, closest

131

to the wick, represents *Malkhut*. The white of the flame represents *Tiferet*. The barely visible, ethereal, colorless, and pure light represents *Binah*. This in turn evokes Shabbat, herself a fusion of the feminine *Malkhut* and the masculine *Tiferet*. Literally over this union there hovers the supernal mother, *Binah*. The Mishnah passage is all about which wicks can be used. The reason the Mishnah is so concerned is because you need a wick that draws the oil. The wick symbolizes our corporeal being, and the oil, the wisdom that flows from above.

7.4 Pieces of Peace

תַּלְמִידֵי חֲכָמִים מַרְבִּים שָׁלוֹם בְּעוֹלָם

Disciples of the sages increase peace in the world.

In his *Olat Reaiyah,* Rabbi Abraham Isaac Kook draws the following insight from the phrase in Mishnah 7, DISCIPLES OF THE SAGES INCREASE PEACE IN THE WORLD: "Puzzled by this awkward construction—How can you 'increase' peace? You either have it or you don't." Kook points out that most people have the mistaken idea that universal peace can only come from universal agreement. They think that peace is the absence of argument, controversy, and contention. For this reason, when they see scholars passionately debating and arguing, each bringing different perspectives, they think that such behavior can only lead away from peace. But in truth, Rav Kook reminds us, real, genuine, and lasting peace can come only from the multiplication of arguments—that all sides and viewpoints are accorded a place at the table, even viewpoints that seem to be in opposition. Only then does peace (and truth and justice) emerge. In this way, each new conflict literally increases the size of the peace, bringing more and more to their seats at the table. In the words of the rabbinic dictum, *Eilu v'eilu divri Elohim chayim,* "These and these (both this and that) are the words of the living God." Now we understand that even obvious contradictions ultimately build the house of reason and enlarge the domain of peace.

7.5 Planned All Along

סוֹף מַעֲשֶׂה בְּמַחֲשָׁבָה תְּחִלָּה

What was last in action was the first in thought.

Commenting on the second verse from *L'khah Dodi*, the Baal Shem Tov (*Siddur Baal Shem Tov*, 326, bottom) offers a comment on how something can be first in thought and last in action, or what philosophers might call the *telos* of creation.

To illustrate his point during a lesson he was teaching, the Baal Shem reached for a pitcher of beer on the table beside him. Holding it up before the class, he reminded them that while the pitcher was only earthenware, it had been shaped by an artisan. Although the clay, the raw material, preceded the pitcher, its present shape was of human intention. Rotating it before his students, he explained how we are able to discern some of the vitality, the creative life force, of the person who made it. We can thus gain an insight into the consciousness of its creator. We can literally feel the mind of the maker in the object. This is echoed in the kabbalistic maxim *ko'al hapo'al ban-ifal*, "The power of the Creator resides in the creation." Then, in an act of great vision, the Baal Shem focused his attention on the simple pitcher of beer itself. "I can see, for instance," he said, "that the artisan who made this had brown hair and a kindly smile; I can see that he had no legs." His students were astonished. "His consciousness, his vitality continues to reside within his creation."

"What would happen," asked a student, "if you were to extract the consciousness of the artist from this vessel?"

"I believe that it would fall apart," replied the teacher.

The lesson concluded, one student remained alone in the room. Curious, he walked up to the table and picked up the pitcher. And, as he did, it disintegrated in his hands! The pitcher had been made, not to hold liquid, but just for the teacher's demonstration, and now it was no longer needed—its artisan's plan fulfilled, its purpose completed.

7.6 The Table

וַיֶּחֱזוּ אֶת־הָאֱלֹהִים וַיֹּאכְלוּ וַיִּשְׁתּוּ

*AND THEY SAW GOD AND THEY ATE
AND THEY DRANK. (Exodus 24:11)*

The Hasidim are fond of citing the verse in Exodus 24:11 describing God's encounter with Moses, Aaron, and the seventy elders, "AND THEY SAW GOD AND THEY ATE AND DRANK," as an indication of the liturgical potential of eating. Not only does the matter (of food) literally become energy, but the Jew who consumes it in holiness effectively frees the holy sparks contained within it. Eating thus becomes a sacred act.

According to Hasidic tradition, the Sabbath table thus becomes more than the mere locus of a meal; it is transformed into an altar evoking the sacrificial altar in the Temple of old. And each Jew therefore becomes a priest performing a sacred ritual. It is not unlike a tea ceremony. Before the Jew are a series of ritual objects, each requiring its own sequence of gestures, melodies, and (for Jews, of course) words. Thus the *challah* is salted in accordance with the verse in Leviticus 2:13, "YOU SHALL SEASON YOUR EVERY OFFERING OF MEAL WITH SALT." Ezekiel 41:22 says, "AN ALTAR OF WOOD, THREE CUBITS HIGH ... AND HE SAID TO ME, 'THIS IS THE TABLE THAT IS BEFORE ADONAI.'" Berakhot 55a notes that the verse opens with "altar" and finishes with "table." Rabbi Yochanan and Rabbi Eleazar both explain that as long as the Temple stood, the altar atoned for Israel, but now one's table makes atonement (cf. Hagigah 27a).

7.7 Messengers

צֵאתְכֶם לְשָׁלוֹם מַלְאֲכֵי הַשָּׁלוֹם

May you go out in peace, messengers of peace.

Shalom Aleikhem first appeared in *Tikkunei Shabbat* (Prague, *1641*). Although it has been adopted with great enthusiasm by Jewish communities throughout the world, it remains the subject of continued controversy and even opposition.

The story of *Shalom Aleikhem* begins with the well-known passage in the Talmud, Shabbat 119b: "Two ministering angels accompany a person on his or her way home from the synagogue on *Erev Shabbat*. One angel is good and one evil. When the person arrives home and finds the Sabbath lamp lit, the table set, and the bed covered with a spread, the good angel exclaims, 'So may it be for another Shabbos too,' and the evil angel has no choice but to answer, 'Amen.' But, if the house has not been prepared for Shabbat, then the evil angel exclaims, 'So may it be for another Shabbat as well,' and the good angel is forced to respond, 'Amen.'"

Several commentators raise questions, however, about the accuracy of the legend. Rabbi Yehuda Aryeh Leib of Ger (d. 1905), author of *Sefat Emet,* points out that there simply are no *bad* ministering angels. Rabbi Jacob Emden (1697–1776) was similarly uncomfortable with any

requests made of angels. Puzzled by the last stanza—
tseitkhem l'shalom, "May you go out in peace …,"—he
asks why should we send angels away. Wouldn't it make
more sense to let them stay with us and rejoice in the
Sabbath meal? Perhaps, Emden suggests, we want them to
leave before something improper takes place, which
might make them leave in anger. Rabbi Hayyim of
Volozhyn (1749–1821) had even stronger reservations.
He writes that it is forbidden to make *any* requests of
angels, for they have no independent power whatsoever.
When a person is worthy, then angels have no choice
but to offer blessing, just as if a person is unworthy,
angels have no choice but to curse. For this reason, the
Volozhyner never recited verse *Barkhuni l'shalom,* "Bless
me for peace." And the Hatam Sofer did not sing *Shalom
Aleikhem* at all, explaining that we are no longer on the
spiritual level to have angels accompany us!

On the other hand, the *Shem Mishmu'el* of Rabbi
Shmuel of Sochtchov notes that all week long a person is
conflicted: the body pulling in one direction, the soul in
another. But on Shabbat, the power of holiness is so
strong that body and soul at last make peace with one
another and, for this reason, the angels bless us. This
seems to imply that the angels represent dimensions of
our own psyches, which, on Shabbat, finally attain a har-
monious balance. Finally, *Siddur Yeshu'at Ya'akov* (Lublin,
1880) advises us that if there is a quarrel in the house and
we refrain from reciting the last stanza, *Tseitkhem
l'shalom,* "May you go out in peace," the quarrel will calm
down *(N'tiv Binah and Be'er Hachasidut, Z'mirot
Shabbat).*

7.8 Children

יְבָרֶכְךָ יְיָ וְיִשְׁמְרֶךָ

MAY ADONAI BLESS YOU AND KEEP YOU.
(Numbers 6:24)

Professor Isadore Twersky of Harvard University, the Talner Rebbe of Boston, once cited Maimonides' son, Avraham Maimuni, saying that when Isaac blesses Jacob (Gen. 27:28), "AND MAY GOD GIVE YOU OF DEW OF HEAVEN, OF FAT OF EARTH ...," the word "and" implies that something has already been spoken *before* the recorded words of the blessing. The actual words of blessing, he concludes, therefore are always preceded by something ineffable. Each blessing begins with something inchoate that can only be inferred or intuited because it is so subtle and sublime. Isaac says earlier in the Genesis story (27:4), "... THAT MY SOUL MAY BLESS YOU...." This reminds us that the main idea of blessing must come from the soul. As Twersky said, the blessings of parent to child are simply too delicate for words.

Johannes Pedersen, in his monumental, four-volume work, *Israel: Its Life and Culture,* (Oxford University Press, Branner Ogkorat, Copenhagen, 1926, vols. 1–2, pp. 198–200), an analysis of the biblical mind, offers a similar and extraordinary insight into the nature of blessing:

"The act of blessing another [*berekh*] means to communicate to [someone] strength of soul, but one can

140

communicate to [another] only of the strength one has in oneself. [One] who blesses another gives [that person] something of his [or her] own soul.... The strength of the word of blessing depends upon the power that the word possesses to hold the real contents of a soul. By means of the word something is laid into the soul of the other...."

Thus, in the case of parents blessing children at the Sabbath table, the core of every blessing is the soul-pride, the sweetness, the *naches,* the parent has received from his or her child over the past week. And, in addition to the formulaic "... like Ephraim and Manasseh" (etc.), parents effectively return the *naches* in words of blessing. The litmus test of the blessing is that it should make the child smile.

Several commentators have attempted to explain why, of all the possible ego models, Ephraim and Manasseh are mentioned by name in the blessing of children. Rabbi Yehuda Aryeh Leib of Ger (d. 1905), author of *Sefat Emet* (1, p. 282 5661), suggests that the reason is that these two sons of Joseph were effectively moved up one generation and treated as children. And this, in turn, reminds us of the direct relationship grandchildren enjoy with their grandparents. Through this grandchild-grandparent bond, we (all) possess an unmediated relationship with our ancestors. Thus, the blessing evokes a direct line to all previous generations. Others have noted that Ephraim and Manasseh, as the first ones born in exile, are symbols of Jewish survival in alien lands. And still others have suggested that Ephraim and Manasseh are mentioned by name because they are the very first set of brothers in the Bible who get along with one another.

7.9 An Extended Hand

כַּפָּהּ פָּרְשָׂה לֶעָנִי
וְיָדֶיהָ שִׁלְּחָה לָאֶבְיוֹן

SHE GIVES GENEROUSLY TO THE POOR;
HER HANDS REACH OUT TO THE NEEDY.
(Proverbs 31:20)

Proverbs 31, known as *ESHET HAYIL*, "A WOMAN OF VALOR"
is customarily sung at the Sabbath table in praise of the
woman of the house by her husband. Rabbi Naftali Tzvi
of Ropschitz, however, used to invert the plain meaning
of verse 20, "HER HANDS REACH OUT TO THE NEEDY" by citing *Leviticus Rabbah* 34 and *Ruth Rabbah* 5:9: "More than
what the householder does for the poor person, the poor
person does for the householder." In simplest terms, when
we have company for dinner, we are on our best behavior.
In this way, even the poorest guest brings good and blessing to the table of the host. And, for this reason, when a
husband chants, "HER HANDS REACH OUT TO THE NEEDY,"
rather than meaning that she does so in generous hospi-
tality, it means she does so in receipt of the gifts created
by simply having any guest at the table.

Professor Elliot Ginsburg of the University of
Michigan notes that, for the kabbalist, the observance of
Shabbat affects the inner life of God. Shabbat becomes

the occasion of a mystical union *within* the Divine. The male dimension, known as *Kudsha B'rikh Hu,* "the Holy One," (corresponding to the *sefirah* of *Tiferet*), unites with the female dimension, known as *Shekhinah,* "the Presence," or *K'nesset Yisrael,* "the community of Israel" (corresponding to the *sefirah* of *Malkhut*). And the chanting of *Eshet Hayil* thus becomes a love song to the *Shekhinah.*

We read in *Zohar* 2:135a–b, a passage known as the *Raza d'Shabbos* ("The Secret of the Sabbath"), or simply by its first Aramaic word, *K'gavna.* It succinctly captures centuries of the Jewish mystical intuition regarding the romance of Shabbat and the role of each Jew in that supernal love. The following is a paraphrase:

Just as they are united on high in the One, so also She is united here below in the secret of the One. Above and below, one corresponding to the other. Even the Holy One who is One is unable to ascend God's throne until She likewise has been transformed through the secret: One with God. And behold, this then is the secret of the only God whose name is One.

And just this is the secret of Shabbat: She is Shabbat concealed within the secret of their One, bringing the secret of the One upon her. And this is the prayer for the entrance of Shabbat: She is the throne of the Presence of the Holy One joined now in the secret of the One. Prepared at last for the Supernal King to dwell upon Her.

When Shabbat enters, She is unique, separate from the "Other Side." And since all judgment is alien to Her, She remains unique in that Holy Light. She is crowned with so many crowns in the presence of the Holy King that all the forces of anger and arrogance of judgment flee; now there is no other ruler throughout all the worlds.

Her face so radiant with that supernal light and crowned here below by a holy people even as all of them are, in turn, blessed with new names. Now commences the prayer to bless Her with joy and faces of light: *Bar'khu et Adonai ham'vorakh....* "Yes, God, Godself, let the window of blessing open onto all creation...."

7.10 Now Finished

וַיְהִי עֶרֶב וַיְהִי בֹקֶר יוֹם הַשִּׁשִּׁי
וַיְכֻלּוּ הַשָּׁמַיִם וְהָאָרֶץ וְכָל צְבָאָם

AND THERE WAS EVENING AND THERE WAS MORNING,
THE SIXTH DAY. AND THE HEAVENS AND THE EARTH WERE
FINISHED AND ALL THEIR HOST. (Genesis 1:31–2:1)

When chanted at home, the *Kiddush* is preceded by the first verses of Genesis 2. They are known by their first word as the VAYKHULU, "AND THEY [THE HEAVENS] WERE FINISHED...." Jewish tradition explains why these three verses are included where they are (that is, at the end of Genesis 1, which details the first six days of creation). The Sabbath, goes Jewish logic, is not another story but an integral part of the creation.

There is an additional custom of prefacing the *vaykhulu* (Gen. 2:1–3) with the final six words of the preceding chapter, VAYHI EREV VAYHI VOKER, YOM HASHISHI, "AND THERE WAS EVENING AND THERE WAS MORNING, THE SIXTH DAY." Although such an addition certainly joins the days of creation with the Sabbath, it also serves a more mystical purpose. The first two words of Genesis 2, VAYKHULU HASHAMAYIM, "AND THE HEAVENS WERE FINISHED ..." begin respectively with the Hebrew letters *vav* and *hey*. By appending the last two words of Genesis 1, YOM HASHISHI,

"THE SIXTH DAY," we add two words whose first letters are, respectively, *yod* and *hey*. Now we have *yod* and *hey* followed by *vav* and *hey*, the tetragrammaton, the awesome four-letter *shem ham'forash*, the ineffable name of God. By joining the work of creation with Sabbath rest, we also reunify the letters of the divine name—hopefully making it and ourselves whole once again.

We also have a tradition from Talmud, Shabbat 119b, that deliberately misreads the word *vaykhulu*. Instead of pronouncing the biblical text (which, of course is not vocalized and thus permits such variations) VAYKHULU, "AND THEY [THE HEAVENS AND THE EARTH] WERE FINISHED," in the *passive* voice, we can also read it as *vay'kalu*, "AND THEY [GOD AND HUMANITY] FINISHED." In this way, just as we have been partners in creation, so do we now become partners in saying *vay'kalu*, "Whew! We're done with our world-work!"

There is a tradition that, while chanting *Kiddush*, one should focus his or her gaze on the Sabbath candles. According to the Talmud (Berakhot 43b; Shabbat 113a), when we run around doing our work during the week, every step takes 1/500th of the light of the eyes or, perhaps, of our mental acuity. But, by gazing at the candles during the recitation of *Kiddush*, our vision, our alertness, our vital energy are renewed and restored.

7.11 Faint with Yearning

הָדוּר נָאֶה זִיו הָעוֹלָם
נַפְשִׁי חוֹלַת אַהֲבָתֶךָ

Radiant brightness of Being; my soul,
faint with your yearning.

A contemporary rendition of *Y'did Nefesh* (from Lawrence Kushner, *The Way Into Jewish Mysticism,* [Woodstock, VT: Jewish Lights, 2001], pp. 46–48) attempts to capture some of the Eros of this extraordinary mystical love poem:

"O Love of my soul, Father of Womb; draw me to Your want, I can run like a deer; reverent toward Your presence, Your love so soft; even sweeter than liquid honey. Radiant brightness of Being; my soul, faint with Your yearning, O God of seeking, heal her; Show her the ecstasy of Your light. Then at last recovery and vigor; now Your servant and forever.

O God, Your longing intimacy; easy please for a child You love, I am only this endless waiting and wanting; just to peek Your Presence, please God, my heart's desire; hurry now with no more hiding.

Show me here Your love; cover me with the shade of Your time. Your Presence lighting the sky; A wedding feast of Your joy, Hurry now my darling, the time is here; loving like long, long ago."

Rabbi Moshe Chayim Epriam of Sudlikov, in his *Degel Machaneh Ephraim (Likkutim),* notes that the word *tsuf,* "honey," in the last line of the first stanza of *Y'did Nefesh,* is similar to one of the words for prophecy, *tsofeh.* Yet so great is our yearning for intimacy with God, he notes, that we choose it not only over honey, but even over being able to foretell the future.

Regarding the phrase in the second stanza *nafshi cholat ahavatecha,* "my soul is faint with your yearning / my soul is lovesick," Rabbi Yoshker Dov of Belz asked his father, Rabbi Joshua of Belz, "Why, if we're lovesick for God, do we want a remedy?"—*El na r'fa na lah,* "Please God, heal her." Shouldn't lovesickness for God be the ultimate goal? His father explained that we're really only requesting that God cure the lovesickness of this *present* moment. This will, however, in turn, create yet a new and more heightened awareness of our distance from God. And, in this way, the absence of intimacy with God will be even more keenly felt. It will serve as an impetus to draw close again.

7.12 Lights of Fire

בּוֹרֵא מְאוֹרֵי הָאֵשׁ

Who creates the lights of fire.

Havdalah and the meal with it, known as a *melaveh malkah* (accompanying the Sabbath queen as she departs), is a time when the boundary between holy and profane is momentarily out of focus. It is also a time, therefore, when life, death, and destiny are a little closer to one another (and our own awareness) than usual. Such imagery appears in many legends.

According to the Talmud (Shabbat 30a), King David begged to know the day of his own death. God agreed and told him that he would die on a Shabbat, but God wouldn't tell him which one! For this reason, *Havdalah* was (needless to say) King David's favorite ceremony: it meant he was assured of living yet another week. In this way, *melaveh malkah* is called "the meal of David."

According to another tradition, Adam was supposed to live for one "God-day," which equals 1,000 years. Yet we read that Adam lived for only 930. This, explains the legend, is because Adam, in a gesture of atonement for his own sin, relinquished 70 of his years to King David. And, because David is of messianic lineage, Adam effectively participates in repairing his own sin.

Even more inventive is a legend explaining that when

149

Adam and Eve ate the fruit, one bone in each of their bodies refused to metabolize the forbidden food, refused to have anything to do with their sin. This bone is called the *luz*-bone. It is also indestructible. Indeed, it is the seed, the physical source, of the body's resurrection. And, says the legend, this stubbornly righteous part of each person's body can be nourished *only* from the food eaten at a *melaveh malkah*.

The *Havdalah* candle has multiple wicks or is braided. Some explain that the reason is because of the blessing recited. According to the school of Shammi, we should say, *borei m'or h'eiysh*, "who creates the *light* of fire" (singular). The school of Hillel, on the other hand (and their opinion is always normative), says the blessing should be *borei m'orei ha'eish*, "who creates the *lights* of fire" (plural).

Tractate Berakhot 52b further notes that the light of fire is composed of white, red, yellow, and blue, which might also explain the reason for a multiwick candle—one wick for each color. Along this same logic, the *Zohar*, commenting on the verse "ADONAI YOUR GOD IS A CONSUMING FIRE …" (Deut. 4:24; 9:3), suggests that multiple wicks would ensure the intermingling of many different colors. Indeed, such a braided candle might create enough individual colors to correspond to each of the ten *sefirot* (emanations or dimensions of the divine psyche) described in the Kabbalah.

While reciting the *Havdalah* blessing over the candle, *borei m'orei ha'eish*, "who creates the lights of fire," it is customary to look at one's fingernails. One legend claims that Adam and Eve's skin was made of nail, which was, in its luminescence, actually able to reflect light. Another tradition suggests that one should see the light of the *Havdalah* candle reflected in his or her fingernails by curling the fingers inward, making an upside-down fist.

The legend goes on to say that our fingertips are supernal lights that illumine and expose each soul's innermost essence. These "tips" of one's innermost soul, like God's presence itself, cannot be seen. Even during this sacred moment of *Havdalah,* we continue to preserve this aspect of holy inwardness.

One final custom bears mention. The braided *Havdalah* candle is extinguished in the wine. According to some, this wine is thereby given special properties. One drop on each eyelash guarantees keen spiritual vision throughout the coming week. (And, while we're at it, one drop in each pocket couldn't be bad for business either!)

7.13 Completion

אֶקְרָא לָאֵל עָלָי גֹמֵר

I CALL UPON THE GOD WHO COMPLETES FOR ME.
(Psalm 57:3)

In his commentary on Psalms, Rabbi Yehuda Aryeh Leib of Ger (d. 1905) reminds us that human beings alone are incapable of completing God's plan. The only true contribution we can make to the whole process is our own humility. Standing in the divine Presence, we acknowledge our own inadequacy, and this "calling upon God," this evoking the divine power, is *our* contribution to ultimate completion. Only God can finish the task. We can only ask for God's help as we begin a new week.

7.14 Elijah

אֵלִיָּהוּ הַנָּבִיא אֵלִיָּהוּ הַתִּשְׁבִּי
אֵלִיָּהוּ הַגִּלְעָדִי

Elijah the prophet, Elijah the Tishbite, Elijah of Gilead.

We have a teaching about Elijah, who is to be the harbinger of the messiah. (Indeed, we sing of Elijah at the conclusion of *Havdalah* in the hopes of persuading the messiah to come—and prolong this Shabbat into eternity.) *Eliyahu hatishbi* means "Elijah, the Tishbite." But, according to the *Ta'amei Haminhagim Um'korei Hadinim* ("The Reasons for Customs and Sources of Laws") of Abraham Isaac Sperling of Lemberg, *hatishbi* is also related to the Hebrew *toshav*, meaning "a resident." This, in turn, initiates a fascinating bit of theology. Each human being—each one of us—is only a *ger*, a stranger who is just "passing through." But since Elijah doesn't die, he and only he lives here eternally—a resident (the only human being without a *luz*-bone).

The story is told of a young man who once journeyed from America to Europe in order to visit the renowned Rabbi Israel Meir Hakohen Kagan (d. 1933), more widely known by the name of his first book, *Hafetz Hayim* ("A Lover of Life"). Upon arriving at the great holy man's apartment, he was astonished by its radical austerity—one room with only a bed, a table, and a chair.

"But where are the rest of your possessions?" asked the young visitor.

The sage replied only with his own question, "And where are yours?"

Flabbergasted, the young man answered, "I don't have any here. I'm only passing through."

"*Nu?*" said the Hafetz Hayim. "So am I."

Inspiration

God in All Moments
Mystical & Practical Spiritual Wisdom from Hasidic Masters
Edited and translated by Or N. Rose with Ebn D. Leader
Hasidic teachings on how to be mindful in religious practice and cultivating everyday ethical behavior—*hanhagot*. 5½ x 8¼, 192 pp, Quality PB, ISBN 1-58023-186-1 **$16.95**

Our Dance with God: Finding Prayer, Perspective and Meaning in the Stories of Our Lives *By Karyn D. Kedar*
Inspiring spiritual insight to guide you on your life journeys and teach you to live and thrive in two conflicting worlds: the rational/material and the spiritual.
6 x 9, 176 pp, Quality PB, ISBN 1-58023-202-7 **$16.99**

The Empty Chair: Finding Hope and Joy—Timeless Wisdom from a Hasidic Master, Rebbe Nachman of Breslov *Adapted by Moshe Mykoff and the Breslov Research Institute*
4 x 6, 128 pp, 2-color text, Deluxe PB w/flaps, ISBN 1-879045-67-2 **$9.95**

The Gentle Weapon: Prayers for Everyday and Not-So-Everyday Moments—Timeless Wisdom from the Teachings of the Hasidic Master, Rebbe Nachman of Breslov
Adapted by Moshe Mykoff and S. C. Mizrahi, together with the Breslov Research Institute
4 x 6, 144 pp, 2-color text, Deluxe PB w/flaps, ISBN 1-58023-022-9 **$9.95**

God Whispers: Stories of the Soul, Lessons of the Heart *By Karyn D. Kedar*
6 x 9, 176 pp, Quality PB, ISBN 1-58023-088-1 **$15.95**

Restful Reflections: Nighttime Inspiration to Calm the Soul, Based on Jewish Wisdom
By Rabbi Kerry M. Olitzky & Rabbi Lori Forman, 4½ x 6¼, 448 pp, Quality PB, ISBN 1-58023-091-1 **$15.95**

Sacred Intentions: Daily Inspiration to Strengthen the Spirit, Based on Jewish Wisdom
By Rabbi Kerry M. Olitzky and Rabbi Lori Forman, 4½ x 6¼, 448 pp, Quality PB, ISBN 1-58023-061-X **$15.95**

Kabbalah/Mysticism/Enneagram

Seek My Face: A Jewish Mystical Theology
By Dr. Arthur Green
This classic work of contemporary Jewish theology, revised and updated.
6 x 9, 304 pp, Quality PB, ISBN 1-58023-130-6 **$19.95**

Zohar: Annotated & Explained
Translation and annotation by Dr. Daniel C. Matt. Foreword by Andrew Harvey
Offers insightful yet unobtrusive commentary to the masterpiece of Jewish mysticism. 5½ x 8¼, 160 pp, Quality PB, ISBN 1-893361-51-9 **$15.99**   *(A SkyLight Paths book)*

Ehyeh: A Kabbalah for Tomorrow *By Dr. Arthur Green*
6 x 9, 224 pp, Quality PB, ISBN 1-58023-213-2 **$16.99;** Hardcover, ISBN 1-58023-125-X **$21.99**

The Enneagram and Kabbalah: Reading Your Soul *By Rabbi Howard A. Addison*
6 x 9, 176 pp, Quality PB, ISBN 1-58023-001-6 **$15.95**

Finding Joy: A Practical Spiritual Guide to Happiness *By Dannel I. Schwartz with Mark Hass*
6 x 9, 192 pp, Quality PB, ISBN 1-58023-009-1 **$14.95;** Hardcover, ISBN 1-879045-53-2 **$19.95**

The Gift of Kabbalah: Discovering the Secrets of Heaven, Renewing Your Life on Earth
By Tamar Frankiel, Ph.D.
6 x 9, 256 pp, Quality PB, ISBN 1-58023-141-1 **$16.95;**
Hardcover, ISBN 1-58023-108-X **$21.95**

The Way Into Jewish Mystical Tradition   *By Lawrence Kushner*
6 x 9, 224 pp, Quality PB, ISBN 1-58023-200-0 **$18.99;** Hardcover, ISBN 1-58023-029-6 **$21.95**

Or phone, fax, mail or e-mail to: **JEWISH LIGHTS** Publishing
Sunset Farm Offices, Route 4 • P.O. Box 237 • Woodstock, Vermont 05091
Tel: (802) 457-4000 • Fax: (802) 457-4004 • www.jewishlights.com
Credit card orders: **(800) 962-4544** (8:30AM–5:30PM ET Monday–Friday)
Generous discounts on quantity orders. SATISFACTION GUARANTEED. Prices subject to change.

Meditation

The Handbook of Jewish Meditation Practices
A Guide for Enriching the Sabbath and Other Days of Your Life
By Rabbi David A. Cooper
Easy-to-learn meditation techniques for use on the Sabbath and every day, to help us return to the roots of traditional Jewish spirituality where Shabbat is a state of mind and soul. 6 x 9, 208 pp, Quality PB, ISBN 1-58023-102-0 **$16.95**

Discovering Jewish Meditation: Instruction & Guidance for Learning an Ancient Spiritual Practice By Nan Fink Gefen, Ph.D.
6 x 9, 208 pp, Quality PB, ISBN 1-58023-067-9 **$16.95**

A Heart of Stillness: A Complete Guide to Learning the Art of Meditation
By Rabbi David A. Cooper
5½ x 8½, 272 pp, Quality PB, ISBN 1-893361-03-9 **$16.95** *(A SkyLight Paths book)*

Meditation from the Heart of Judaism: Today's Teachers Share Their Practices, Techniques, and Faith Edited by Avram Davis
6 x 9, 256 pp, Quality PB, ISBN 1-58023-049-0 **$16.95**

Silence, Simplicity & Solitude: A Complete Guide to Spiritual Retreat at Home
By Rabbi David A. Cooper
5½ x 8½, 336 pp, Quality PB, ISBN 1-893361-04-7 **$16.95** *(A SkyLight Paths book)*

Three Gates to Meditation Practice: A Personal Journey into Sufism, Buddhism, and Judaism By Rabbi David A. Cooper
5½ x 8½, 240 pp, Quality PB, ISBN 1-893361-22-5 **$16.95** *(A SkyLight Paths book)*

The Way of Flame: A Guide to the Forgotten Mystical Tradition of Jewish Meditation
By Avram Davis 4½ x 8, 176 pp, Quality PB, ISBN 1-58023-060-1 **$15.95**

Ritual/Sacred Practice/Journaling

The Jewish Dream Book: The Key to Opening the Inner Meaning of Your Dreams By Vanessa L. Ochs with Elizabeth Ochs; Full-color illus. by Kristina Swarner
Instructions for how modern people can perform ancient Jewish dream practices and dream interpretations drawn from the Jewish wisdom tradition. For anyone who wants to understand their dreams—and themselves.
8 x 8, 120 pp, Full-color illus., Deluxe PB w/flaps, ISBN 1-58023-132-2 **$16.95**

The Jewish Journaling Book: How to Use Jewish Tradition to Write Your Life & Explore Your Soul By Janet Ruth Falon
Details the history of Jewish journaling throughout biblical and modern times, and teaches specific journaling techniques to help you create and maintain a vital journal, from a Jewish perspective. 8 x 8, 304 pp, Deluxe PB w/flaps, ISBN 1-58023-203-5 **$18.99**

The Rituals & Practices of a Jewish Life: A Handbook for Personal Spiritual Renewal Edited by Rabbi Kerry M. Olitzky and Rabbi Daniel Judson
6 x 9, 272 pp, illus., Quality PB, ISBN 1-58023-169-1 **$18.95**

The Book of Jewish Sacred Practices: CLAL's Guide to Everyday & Holiday Rituals & Blessings Edited by Rabbi Irwin Kula and Vanessa L. Ochs, Ph.D.
6 x 9, 368 pp, Quality PB, ISBN 1-58023-152-7 **$18.95**

Science Fiction/ Mystery & Detective Fiction

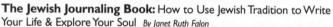

Mystery Midrash: An Anthology of Jewish Mystery & Detective Fiction
Edited by Lawrence W. Raphael. Preface by Joel Siegel.
6 x 9, 304 pp, Quality PB, ISBN 1-58023-055-5 **$16.95**

Criminal Kabbalah: An Intriguing Anthology of Jewish Mystery & Detective Fiction
Edited by Lawrence W. Raphael. Foreword by Laurie R. King.
6 x 9, 256 pp, Quality PB, ISBN 1-58023-109-8 **$16.95**

More Wandering Stars: An Anthology of Outstanding Stories of Jewish Fantasy and Science Fiction Edited by Jack Dann. Introduction by Isaac Asimov.
6 x 9, 192 pp, Quality PB, ISBN 1-58023-063-6 **$16.95**

Wandering Stars: An Anthology of Jewish Fantasy & Science Fiction
Edited by Jack Dann. Introduction by Isaac Asimov.
6 x 9, 272 pp, Quality PB, ISBN 1-58023-005-9 **$16.95**

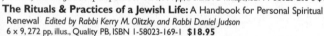

Spirituality

The Alphabet of Paradise: An A–Z of Spirituality for Everyday Life
By Rabbi Howard Cooper
In twenty-six engaging chapters, Cooper spiritually illuminates the subjects of our daily lives—A to Z—examining these sources by using an ancient Jewish mystical method of interpretation that reveals both the literal and more allusive meanings of each. 5 x 7¼, 224 pp, Quality PB, ISBN 1-893361-80-2 **$16.95** *(A SkyLight Paths book)*

Does the Soul Survive?: A Jewish Journey to Belief in Afterlife, Past Lives & Living with Purpose *By Rabbi Elie Kaplan Spitz. Foreword by Brian L. Weiss, M.D.*
Spitz relates his own experiences and those shared with him by people he has worked with as a rabbi, and shows us that belief in afterlife and past lives, so often approached with reluctance, is in fact true to Jewish tradition.
6 x 9, 288 pp, Quality PB, ISBN 1-58023-165-9 **$16.95**; Hardcover, ISBN 1-58023-094-6 **$21.95**

First Steps to a New Jewish Spirit: Reb Zalman's Guide to Recapturing the Intimacy & Ecstasy in Your Relationship with God
By Rabbi Zalman M. Schachter-Shalomi with Donald Gropman
An extraordinary spiritual handbook that restores psychic and physical vigor by introducing us to new models and alternative ways of practicing Judaism. Offers meditation and contemplation exercises for enriching the most important aspects of everyday life. 6 x 9, 144 pp, Quality PB, ISBN 1-58023-182-9 **$16.95**

God in Our Relationships: Spirituality between People from the Teachings of Martin Buber *By Rabbi Dennis S. Ross*
On the eightieth anniversary of Buber's classic work, we can discover new answers to critical issues in our lives. Inspiring examples from Ross's own life— as congregational rabbi, father, hospital chaplain, social worker, and husband— illustrate Buber's difficult-to-understand ideas about how we encounter God and each other. 5½ x 8½, 160 pp, Quality PB, ISBN 1-58023-147-0 **$16.95**

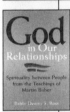

The Jewish Lights Spirituality Handbook: A Guide to Understanding, Exploring & Living a Spiritual Life *Edited by Stuart M. Matlins*
What exactly is "Jewish" about spirituality? How do I make it a part of my life? Fifty of today's foremost spiritual leaders share their ideas and experience with us.
6 x 9, 456 pp, Quality PB, ISBN 1-58023-093-8 **$19.99**; Hardcover, ISBN 1-58023-100-4 **$24.95**

Bringing the Psalms to Life: How to Understand and Use the Book of Psalms
By Dr. Daniel F. Polish
6 x 9, 208 pp, Quality PB, ISBN 1-58023-157-8 **$16.95**; Hardcover, ISBN 1-58023-077-6 **$21.95**

God & the Big Bang: Discovering Harmony between Science & Spirituality
By Dr. Daniel C. Matt 6 x 9, 216 pp, Quality PB, ISBN 1-879045-89-3 **$16.95**

Godwrestling—Round 2: Ancient Wisdom, Future Paths
By Rabbi Arthur Waskow 6 x 9, 352 pp, Quality PB, ISBN 1-879045-72-9 **$18.95**

One God Clapping: The Spiritual Path of a Zen Rabbi *By Rabbi Alan Lew with Sherril Jaffe*
5½ x 8½, 336 pp, Quality PB, ISBN 1-58023-115-2 **$16.95**

The Path of Blessing: Experiencing the Energy and Abundance of the Divine
By Rabbi Marcia Prager 5½ x 8½, 240 pp, Quality PB, ISBN 1-58023-148-9 **$16.95**

Six Jewish Spiritual Paths: A Rationalist Looks at Spirituality *By Rabbi Rifat Sonsino*
6 x 9, 208 pp, Quality PB, ISBN 1-58023-167-5 **$16.95**; Hardcover, ISBN 1-58023-095-4 **$21.95**

Soul Judaism: Dancing with God into a New Era
By Rabbi Wayne Dosick 5½ x 8½, 304 pp, Quality PB, ISBN 1-58023-053-9 **$16.95**

Stepping Stones to Jewish Spiritual Living: Walking the Path Morning, Noon, and Night *By Rabbi James L. Mirel and Karen Bonnell Werth*
6 x 9, 240 pp, Quality PB, ISBN 1-58023-074-1 **$16.95**; Hardcover, ISBN 1-58023-003-2 **$21.95**

There Is No Messiah... and You're It: The Stunning Transformation of Judaism's Most Provocative Idea *By Rabbi Robert N. Levine, D.D.*
6 x 9, 192 pp, Hardcover, ISBN 1-58023-173-X **$21.95**

These Are the Words: A Vocabulary of Jewish Spiritual Life *By Dr. Arthur Green*
6 x 9, 304 pp, Quality PB, ISBN 1-58023-107-1 **$18.95**

Theology/Philosophy

Aspects of Rabbinic Theology
By Solomon Schechter. New Introduction by Dr. Neil Gillman.
6 x 9, 448 pp, Quality PB, ISBN 1-879045-24-9 **$19.95**

Broken Tablets: Restoring the Ten Commandments and Ourselves
Edited by Rachel S. Mikva. Introduction by Lawrence Kushner. Afterword by Arnold Jacob Wolf.
6 x 9, 192 pp, Quality PB, ISBN 1-58023-158-6 **$16.95**; Hardcover, ISBN 1-58023-066-0 **$21.95**

Creating an Ethical Jewish Life
A Practical Introduction to Classic Teachings on How to Be a Jew
By Dr. Byron L. Sherwin and Seymour J. Cohen
6 x 9, 336 pp, Quality PB, ISBN 1-58023-114-4 **$19.95**

The Death of Death: Resurrection and Immortality in Jewish Thought
By Dr. Neil Gillman   6 x 9, 336 pp, Quality PB, ISBN 1-58023-081-4 **$18.95**

Evolving Halakhah: A Progressive Approach to Traditional Jewish Law
By Rabbi Dr. Moshe Zemer
6 x 9, 480 pp, Quality PB, ISBN 1-58023-127-6 **$29.95**; Hardcover, ISBN 1-58023-002-4 **$40.00**

Hasidic Tales: Annotated & Explained
By Rabbi Rami Shapiro. Foreword by Andrew Harvey, SkyLight Illuminations series editor.
5½ x 8½, 240 pp, Quality PB, ISBN 1-893361-86-1 **$16.95** (A SkyLight Paths book)

A Heart of Many Rooms: Celebrating the Many Voices within Judaism
By Dr. David Hartman 6 x 9, 352 pp, Quality PB, ISBN 1-58023-156-X **$19.95**

The Hebrew Prophets: Selections Annotated & Explained
Translation & Annotation by Rabbi Rami Shapiro. Foreword by Zalman M. Schachter-Shalomi.
5½ x 8½, 224 pp, Quality PB, ISBN 1-59473-037-7 **$16.99** (A SkyLight Paths book)

Keeping Faith with the Psalms: Deepen Your Relationship with God Using the
Book of Psalms By Daniel F. Polish 6 x 9, 272 pp, Hardcover, ISBN 1-58023-179-9 **$24.95**

The Last Trial
On the Legends and Lore of the Command to Abraham to Offer Isaac as a Sacrifice
By Shalom Spiegel. New Introduction by Judah Goldin.
6 x 9, 208 pp, Quality PB, ISBN 1-879045-29-X **$18.95**

A Living Covenant: The Innovative Spirit in Traditional Judaism
By Dr. David Hartman 6 x 9, 368 pp, Quality PB, ISBN 1-58023-011-3 **$18.95**

Love and Terror in the God Encounter
The Theological Legacy of Rabbi Joseph B. Soloveitchik
By Dr. David Hartman
6 x 9, 240 pp, Quality PB, ISBN 1-58023-176-4 **$19.95**; Hardcover, ISBN 1-58023-112-8 **$25.00**

Seeking the Path to Life
Theological Meditations on God and the Nature of People, Love, Life and Death
By Rabbi Ira F. Stone 6 x 9, 160 pp, Quality PB, ISBN 1-879045-47-8 **$14.95**

The Spirit of Renewal: Finding Faith after the Holocaust
By Rabbi Edward Feld 6 x 9, 224 pp, Quality PB, ISBN 1-879045-40-0 **$16.95**

Tormented Master: The Life and Spiritual Quest of Rabbi Nahman of Bratslav
By Dr. Arthur Green 6 x 9, 416 pp, Quality PB, ISBN 1-879045-11-7 **$19.99**

Your Word Is Fire: The Hasidic Masters on Contemplative Prayer
Edited and translated by Dr. Arthur Green and Barry W. Holtz
6 x 9, 160 pp, Quality PB, ISBN 1-879045-25-7 **$15.95**

I Am Jewish
Personal Reflections Inspired by the Last Words of Daniel Pearl
Almost 150 Jews—both famous and not—from all walks of life, from all around
the world, write about Identity, Heritage, Covenant / Chosenness and Faith,
Humanity and Ethnicity, and *Tikkun Olam* and Justice.
Edited by Judea and Ruth Pearl
6 x 9, 304 pp, Hardcover, ISBN 1-58023-183-7 **$24.99**

Download a free copy of the *I Am Jewish Teacher's Guide* at our website:
www.jewishlights.com

Spirituality/Women's Interest

The Quotable Jewish Woman: Wisdom, Inspiration & Humor from the Mind & Heart *Edited and compiled by Elaine Bernstein Partnow*
The definitive collection of ideas, reflections, humor, and wit of over 300 Jewish women. 6 x 9, 496 pp, Hardcover, ISBN 1-58023-193-4 **$29.99**

Lifecycles, Vol. 1: Jewish Women on Life Passages & Personal Milestones
Edited and with introductions by Rabbi Debra Orenstein 6 x 9, 480 pp, Quality PB, ISBN 1-58023-018-0 **$19.95**

Lifecycles, Vol. 2: Jewish Women on Biblical Themes in Contemporary Life
Edited and with introductions by Rabbi Debra Orenstein and Rabbi Jane Rachel Litman
6 x 9, 464 pp, Quality PB, ISBN 1-58023-019-9 **$19.95**

Moonbeams: A Hadassah Rosh Hodesh Guide *Edited by Carol Diament, Ph.D.*
8½ x 11, 240 pp, Quality PB, ISBN 1-58023-099-7 **$20.00**

ReVisions: Seeing Torah through a Feminist Lens *By Rabbi Elyse Goldstein*
5½ x 8½, 224 pp, Quality PB, ISBN 1-58023-117-9 **$16.95**

White Fire: A Portrait of Women Spiritual Leaders in America
By Rabbi Malka Drucker. Photographs by Gay Block.
7 x 10, 320 pp, 30+ b/w photos, Hardcover, ISBN 1-893361-64-0 **$24.95** *(A SkyLight Paths book)*

Women of the Wall: Claiming Sacred Ground at Judaism's Holy Site
Edited by Phyllis Chesler and Rivka Haut 6 x 9, 496 pp, b/w photos, Hardcover, ISBN 1-58023-161-6 **$34.95**

The Women's Haftarah Commentary: New Insights from Women Rabbis on the 54 Weekly Haftarah Portions, the 5 Megillot & Special Shabbatot
Edited by Rabbi Elyse Goldstein 6 x 9, 560 pp, Hardcover, ISBN 1-58023-133-0 **$39.99**

The Women's Passover Companion: Women's Reflections on the Festival of Freedom *Edited by Rabbi Sharon Cohen Aisfeld, Tara Mohr, and Catherine Spector*
6 x 9, 352 pp, Hardcover, ISBN 1-58023-128-4 **$24.95**

The Women's Seder Sourcebook: Rituals and Readings for Use at the Passover Seder *Edited by Rabbi Sharon Cohen Aisfeld, Tara Mohr, and Catherine Spector*
6 x 9, 384 pp, Hardcover, ISBN 1-58023-136-5 **$24.95**

The Women's Torah Commentary: New Insights from Women Rabbis on the 54 Weekly Torah Portions *Edited by Rabbi Elyse Goldstein*
6 x 9, 496 pp, Hardcover, ISBN 1-58023-076-8 **$34.95**

The Year Mom Got Religion: One Woman's Midlife Journey into Judaism
By Lee Meyerhoff Hendler 6 x 9, 208 pp, Quality PB, ISBN 1-58023-070-9 **$15.95**

Travel

Israel—A Spiritual Travel Guide: A Companion for the Modern Jewish Pilgrim
By Rabbi Lawrence A. Hoffman 4¾ x 10, 256 pp, Quality PB, illus., ISBN 1-879045-56-7 **$18.95**
Also Available: **The Israel Mission Leader's Guide** ISBN 1-58023-085-7 **$4.95**

12 Steps

100 Blessings Every Day
Daily Twelve Step Recovery Affirmations, Exercises for Personal Growth & Renewal Reflecting Seasons of the Jewish Year
By Rabbi Kerry M. Olitzky. Foreword by Rabbi Neil Gillman.
One-day-at-a-time monthly format. Reflects on the rhythm of the Jewish calendar to bring insight to recovery from addictions.
4½ x 6½, 432 pp, Quality PB, ISBN 1-879045-30-3 **$15.99**

Recovery from Codependence: A Jewish Twelve Steps Guide to Healing Your Soul
By Rabbi Kerry M. Olitzky 6 x 9, 160 pp, Quality PB, ISBN 1-879045-32-X **$13.95**

Renewed Each Day: Daily Twelve Step Recovery Meditations Based on the Bible
By Rabbi Kerry M. Olitzky and Aaron Z.
Vol. 1—Genesis & Exodus: 6 x 9, 224 pp, Quality PB, ISBN 1-879045-12-5 **$14.95**
Vol. 2—Leviticus, Numbers & Deuteronomy: 6 x 9, 280 pp, Quality PB, ISBN 1-879045-13-3 **$14.95**

Twelve Jewish Steps to Recovery: A Personal Guide to Turning from Alcoholism & Other Addictions—Drugs, Food, Gambling, Sex...
By Rabbi Kerry M. Olitzky and Stuart A. Copans, M.D. Preface by Abraham J. Twerski, M.D.
6 x 9, 144 pp, Quality PB, ISBN 1-879045-09-5 **$14.95**

Spirituality/The Way Into... Series

The Way Into... Series offers an accessible and highly usable "guided tour" of the Jewish faith, people, history and beliefs—in total, an introduction to Judaism that will enable you to understand and interact with the sacred texts of the Jewish tradition. Each volume is written by a leading contemporary scholar and teacher, and explores one key aspect of Judaism. *The Way Into...* enables all readers to achieve a real sense of Jewish cultural literacy through guided study.

The Way Into Encountering God in Judaism *By Neil Gillman*
6 x 9, 240 pp, Quality PB, ISBN 1-58023-199-3 **$18.99**; Hardcover, ISBN 1-58023-025-3 **$21.95**

Also Available: **The Jewish Approach to God: A Brief Introduction for Christians**
By Neil Gillman 5½ x 8½, 192 pp, Quality PB, ISBN 1-58023-190-X **$16.95**

The Way Into Jewish Mystical Tradition *By Lawrence Kushner*
6 x 9, 224 pp, Quality PB, ISBN 1-58023-200-0 **$18.99**; Hardcover, ISBN 1-58023-029-6 **$21.95**

The Way Into Jewish Prayer *By Lawrence A. Hoffman*
6 x 9, 224 pp, Quality PB, ISBN 1-58023-201-9 **$18.99**; Hardcover, ISBN 1-58023-027-X **$21.95**

The Way Into Torah *By Norman J. Cohen*
6 x 9, 176 pp, Quality PB, ISBN 1-58023-198-5 **$16.99**; Hardcover, ISBN 1-58023-028-8 **$21.95**

Spirituality in the Workplace

Being God's Partner
How to Find the Hidden Link Between Spirituality and Your Work
By Rabbi Jeffrey K. Salkin. Introduction by Norman Lear.
6 x 9, 192 pp, Quality PB, ISBN 1-879045-65-6 **$17.95**

The Business Bible: 10 New Commandments for Bringing Spirituality & Ethical
Values into the Workplace *By Rabbi Wayne Dosick*
5½ x 8½, 208 pp, Quality PB, ISBN 1-58023-101-2 **$14.95**

Spirituality and Wellness

Aleph-Bet Yoga
Embodying the Hebrew Letters for Physical and Spiritual Well-Being
By Steven A. Rapp. Foreword by Tamar Frankiel, Ph.D., and Judy Greenfeld. Preface by Hart Lazer.
7 x 10, 128 pp, b/w photos, Quality PB, Layflat binding, ISBN 1-58023-162-4 **$16.95**

Entering the Temple of Dreams
Jewish Prayers, Movements, and Meditations for the End of the Day
By Tamar Frankiel, Ph.D., and Judy Greenfeld
7 x 10, 192 pp, illus., Quality PB, ISBN 1-58023-079-2 **$16.95**

Jewish Paths toward Healing and Wholeness: A Personal Guide to Dealing
with Suffering *By Rabbi Kerry M. Olitzky. Foreword by Debbie Friedman.*
6 x 9, 192 pp, Quality PB, ISBN 1-58023-068-7 **$15.95**

Minding the Temple of the Soul
Balancing Body, Mind, and Spirit through Traditional Jewish Prayer, Movement, and
Meditation *By Tamar Frankiel, Ph.D., and Judy Greenfeld*
7 x 10, 184 pp, illus., Quality PB, ISBN 1-879045-64-8 **$16.95**
Audiotape of the Blessings and Meditations: 60 min. **$9.95**
Videotape of the Movements and Meditations: 46 min. **$20.00**

Spirituality/Lawrence Kushner

The Book of Letters: A Mystical Hebrew Alphabet
Popular Hardcover Edition, 6 x 9, 80 pp, 2-color text, ISBN 1-879045-00-1 **$24.95**
Deluxe Gift Edition with slipcase, 9 x 12, 80 pp, 4-color text, Hardcover, ISBN 1-879045-01-X **$79.95**
Collector's Limited Edition, 9 x 12, 80 pp, gold foil embossed pages, w/limited edition silkscreened
print, ISBN 1-879045-04-4 **$349.00**

The Book of Miracles: A Young Person's Guide to Jewish Spiritual Awareness
All-new illustrations by the author
6 x 9, 96 pp, 2-color illus., Hardcover, ISBN 1-879045-78-8 **$16.95** *For ages 9–13*

The Book of Words: Talking Spiritual Life, Living Spiritual Talk
6 x 9, 160 pp, Quality PB, ISBN 1-58023-020-2 **$16.95**

Eyes Remade for Wonder: A Lawrence Kushner Reader
Introduction by Thomas Moore
6 x 9, 240 pp, Quality PB, ISBN 1-58023-042-3 **$18.95;** Hardcover, ISBN 1-58023-014-8 **$23.95**

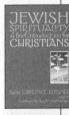

God Was in This Place & I, i Did Not Know
Finding Self, Spirituality and Ultimate Meaning
6 x 9, 192 pp, Quality PB, ISBN 1-879045-33-8 **$16.95**

Honey from the Rock: An Introduction to Jewish Mysticism
6 x 9, 176 pp, Quality PB, ISBN 1-58023-073-3 **$16.95**

Invisible Lines of Connection: Sacred Stories of the Ordinary
5½ x 8½, 160 pp, Quality PB, ISBN 1-879045-98-2 **$15.95**

Jewish Spirituality—A Brief Introduction for Christians
5½ x 8½, 112 pp, Quality PB Original, ISBN 1-58023-150-0 **$12.95**

The River of Light: Jewish Mystical Awareness
6 x 9, 192 pp, Quality PB, ISBN 1-58023-096-2 **$16.95**

The Way Into Jewish Mystical Tradition
6 x 9, 224 pp, Quality PB, ISBN 1-58023-200-0 **$18.99;** Hardcover, ISBN 1-58023-029-6 **$21.95**

Spirituality/Prayer

Pray Tell: A Hadassah Guide to Jewish Prayer
By Rabbi Jules Harlow, with contributions from Tamara Cohen, Rochelle Furstenberg, Rabbi Daniel Gordis, Leora Tanenbaum, and many others
A guide to traditional Jewish prayer enriched with insight and wisdom from a broad variety of viewpoints—from Orthodox, Conservative, Reform, and Reconstructionist Judaism to New Age and feminist.
8½ x 11, 400 pp, Quality PB, ISBN 1-58023-163-2 **$29.95**

My People's Prayer Book Series
Traditional Prayers, Modern Commentaries
Edited by Rabbi Lawrence A. Hoffman
Provides diverse and exciting commentary to the traditional liturgy, helping modern men and women find new wisdom in Jewish prayer, and bring liturgy into their lives. Each book includes Hebrew text, modern translation, and commentaries from all perspectives of the Jewish world.

Vol. 1—The *Sh'ma* and Its Blessings
7 x 10, 168 pp, Hardcover, ISBN 1-879045-79-6 **$23.95**
Vol. 2—The *Amidah*
7 x 10, 240 pp, Hardcover, ISBN 1-879045-80-X **$24.95**
Vol. 3—*P'sukei D'zimrah* (Morning Psalms)
7 x 10, 240 pp, Hardcover, ISBN 1-879045-81-8 **$24.95**
Vol. 4—*Seder K'riat Hatorah* (The Torah Service)
7 x 10, 264 pp, Hardcover, ISBN 1-879045-82-6 **$23.95**
Vol. 5—*Birkhot Hashachar* (Morning Blessings)
7 x 10, 240 pp, Hardcover, ISBN 1-879045-83-4 **$24.95**
Vol. 6—*Tachanun* and Concluding Prayers
7 x 10, 240 pp, Hardcover, ISBN 1-879045-84-2 **$24.95**
Vol. 7—Shabbat at Home
7 x 10, 240 pp, Hardcover, ISBN 1-879045-85-0 **$24.95**
Vol. 8—*Kabbalat Shabbat* (Welcoming Shabbat in the Synagogue)
7 x 10, 240 pp (est), Hardcover, ISBN 1-58023-121-7 **$24.99**

About Jewish Lights

People of all faiths and backgrounds yearn for books that attract, engage, educate, and spiritually inspire.

Our principal goal is to stimulate thought and help all people learn about who the Jewish People are, where they come from, and what the future can be made to hold. While people of our diverse Jewish heritage are the primary audience, our books speak to people in the Christian world as well and will broaden their understanding of Judaism and the roots of their own faith.

We bring to you authors who are at the forefront of spiritual thought and experience. While each has something different to say, they all say it in a voice that you can hear.

Our books are designed to welcome you and then to engage, stimulate, and inspire. We judge our success not only by whether or not our books are beautiful and commercially successful, but by whether or not they make a difference in your life.

For your information and convenience, at the back of this book we have provided a list of other Jewish Lights books you might find interesting and useful. They cover all the categories of your life:

Bar/Bat Mitzvah
Bible Study / Midrash
Children's Books
Congregation Resources
Current Events / History
Ecology
Fiction: Mystery, Science Fiction
Grief / Healing
Holidays / Holy Days
Inspiration
Kabbalah / Mysticism / Enneagram

Life Cycle
Meditation
Parenting
Prayer
Ritual / Sacred Practice
Spirituality
Theology / Philosophy
Travel
Twelve Steps
Women's Interest

Stuart M. Matlins, Publisher

Or phone, fax, mail or e-mail to: **JEWISH LIGHTS Publishing**
Sunset Farm Offices, Route 4 • P.O. Box 237 • Woodstock, Vermont 05091
Tel: (802) 457-4000 • Fax: (802) 457-4004 • www.jewishlights.com
Credit card orders: **(800) 962-4544** (8:30AM–5:30PM ET Monday–Friday)
Generous discounts on quantity orders. SATISFACTION GUARANTEED. Prices subject to change.

**For more information about each book,
visit our website at www.jewishlights.com**